REA

Educ   outh

The In   erience

Education Policy Perspectives

General Editor: Professor Ivor Goodson, Faculty of Education, University of Western Ontario, London, Canada N6G 1G7

Education policy analysis has long been a neglected area in the United Kingdom and, to an extent, in the USA and Australia. The result has been a profound gap between the study of education and the formulation of education policy. For practitioners such a lack of analysis of the new policy initiatives has worrying implications particularly at such a time of policy flux and change. Education policy has, in recent years, been a matter for intense political debate — the political and public interest in the working of the system has come at the same time as the consensus on education policy has been broken by the advent of the 'New Right'. As never before the political parties and pressure groups differ in their articulated policies and prescriptions for the education sector. Critical thinking about these developments is clearly necessary.

All those working within the system also need information on policy making, policy implementation and effective day-to-day operation. Pressure on schools from government, education authorities and parents has generated an enormous need for knowledge amongst those on the receiving end of educational policies.

This series aims to fill the academic gap, to reflect the politicalization of education, and to provide the practitioners with the analysis for informed implementation of policies that they will need. It will offer studies in broad areas of policy studies. Beside the general section it will offer a particular focus in the following areas: School organization and improvement (David Reynolds, University College, Cardiff, UK); Critical social analysis (Professor Philip Wexler, University of Rochester, USA); Policy studies and evaluation (Professor Ernest House, University of Colorado-Boulder, USA); and Education and training (Dr Peter Cuttance, University of Edinburgh, UK).

Education Policy Perspectives

Education and American Youth
The Impact of the High School Experience

Ruth B. Ekstrom, Margaret E. Goertz
and Donald A. Rock

 The Falmer Press

(A member of the Taylor & Francis Group)
London · New York · Philadelphia

USA	The Falmer Press, Taylor & Francis Inc., 242 Cherry Street, Philadelphia, PA 19106–1906
UK	The Falmer Press, Falmer House, Barcombe, Lewes, East Sussex, BN8 5DL

Copyright © Educational Testing Service, 1988

First published 1988

Library of Congress Cataloging-in-Publication Data

Ekstrom, Ruth B.
    Education and Amreican youth : the impact of the high school experience / Ruth B. Ekstrom, Margaret E. Goertz, and Donald A. Rock.
        p. cm.—(Education policy perspectives)
       Bibliography: p.
       Includes index.
       ISBN 1–85000–375–0 : (U.S.).   ISBN 1–85000–376–9 (pbk.) : (U.S.)
       1. High schools—United States—Longitudinal studies. 2. High school students—United States—Longitudinal studies. I. Goertz, Margaret E. II. Rock, Donald A. III. Title. IV. Series.
LA22.E39 1988
373.18′0973—dc19   87–35990
                                                      CIP

Jacket design by Caroline Archer

Typeset in 11/13 Bembo by
Imago Publishing Ltd, Thame, Oxon

*Printed and bound in Great Britain by
Redwood Burn Limited, Trowbridge, Wiltshire.*

Contents

List of Tables

Preface

This book is the outgrowth of two studies conducted by the authors for the United States Department of Education's Center for Statistics. Known as the *Study of Excellence in High School Education*, they included: (i) a cross-sectional analysis comparing 1972 and 1980 high school seniors and their schools; and (ii) a longitudinal analysis relating cognitive growth of 1980 high school sophomores to their schooling experiences over the period 1980 to 1982. The general, long-term goal of these two studies was to provide information that would improve school quality and, thus, produce excellence in high school education.

The major objectives of the cross-sectional study were to: (i) document changes in achievement and other student outcomes over time, both nationally and by selected subpopulations, between 1972 and 1980; (ii) identify the school and student variables that are related to changes in student achievement and other outcomes; and (iii) present this information to educational policymakers in a way that would illuminate and assist their decision making.

The major objectives of the longitudinal study were to: (i) document changes in student achievement, attitudes, behaviors and values between the sophomore and senior years in high school; (ii) identify the school-related and student-related variables that affected changes in student outcomes; (iii) understand how these variables and the interaction among them affect the quality of high school education; and (iv) present this information to educational policymakers in a way that would illuminate and assist their decision making and lead to excellence in high school education.

In this volume we have extended our cross-sectional analysis to compare the experiences and tested achievement of high school seniors over the decade 1972 to 1982. The longitudinal analysis was enriched by an in-depth look at growth in different kinds of mathematical skills acquired during the last two years of high school. In addition, we broadened the focus of our analysis to include an examination of student access to those educational processes shown to contribute most to achievement growth.

The chapter on dropouts first appeared in *School Dropouts: Patterns and Policies*, edited by Gary Natriello and published by Teachers College Press. A summary of the findings relating to student achievement appeared in *The Contributions of the Social Sciences to Educational Policy and Practice: 1965–1985*, edited by Jane Hannaway and Marlaine Lockheed and published by McCutchan Publishing Company.

Our initial research was made possible by a grant from the United States Department of Education. Several staff members of the Center for Statistics, in particular William Fetters, Dennis Carroll and Jeffrey Owings, made valuable contributions to our work. Educational Testing Service provided funds for additional data analyses and for our time to write this book. Ernie Anastasio, C. V. Bunderson, Joan Baratz-Snowden and Henry Braun were instrumental in our receiving this support.

We owe a special debt to Judith Pollack who patiently and expertly coped with our many requests for data analysis and kept track of the many different data sets and variables. Without Judy's expertise in programming this data-based book could never have been written.

The conclusions in this book are, of course, our own and do not necessarily reflect the policies or opinions of the United States Department of Education or Educational Testing Service.

PART 1
EDUCATION AND AMERICAN YOUTH:
THE IMPACT OF THE HIGH SCHOOL
EXPERIENCE — AN INTRODUCTION

1   *Introduction*

This is a book about excellence, equity and choice in American secondary education. It examines policy issues in each of these areas that have been raised by the educational reform movement of the 1980s. Has the quality of education in the American high school deteriorated? Why are students dropping out of high school? What can schools do to retain more students? How do educational experiences differ in public and private schools? What factors contribute to academic achievement in the high school? Do all students have equal access to learning opportunities that encourage educational attainment?

We use data from two nationally representative surveys of high school students conducted by the Center for Statistics of the United States Department of Education — the National Longitudinal Survey of 1972 (NLS-72) and High School and Beyond (HS&B) — to address these questions. Part 2 of the book describes changes in American high schools and their students between 1972 and 1982 and discusses how these changes are related to the widely-heralded test score declines of the period. In Part 3, we focus on factors that appear to contribute to achievement and persistence during the last two years of high school. We conduct separate analyses for students by sex, race/ethnicity, socioeconomic status, school type and school curriculum to investigate whether educational processes work the same for all students and to determine which students have access to beneficial processes. We conclude the book with a discussion of the implications of these findings for policies that will increase equity and excellence in American schools.

This introductory part serves three purposes. First, it describes the context for the current debate over excellence, equity and choice in education. Second, it summarizes the body of research underlying studies of determinants of achievement. Finally, it provides an over-view of the book and the study methodology.

The Context of the Education Reform Movement of the 1980s

A tension between the values of equity, excellence and choice has characterized education reform movements in the United States for the last one hundred years.

> In conservative times — in the 1890s, the 1950s, and the 1980s, for example — the keynotes of 'reform' have typically been a focus on the talented, calls for greater emphasis on the basics and greater stress on academics in general, and concern about incoherence in curriculum and a lack of discipline... By con-trast, in more liberal eras — the progressive decades, the 1930s, the 1960s, or the early 1970s —'attention shifted to the 'disadvantaged' and to broadening the functions of schooling.[1]

The focus in the early stages of the education reform movement of the 1980s was on excellence. As noted in the quotation above, recom-mendations emphasized higher educational standards: more course work, particularly in the 'New Basics'; more homework; longer school days; better teachers and higher levels of minimum proficiency. A renewed interest in issues of equity emerged in 1987, however, as states began to address the problems of persistent dropout rates and differential performance between minority and majority students. Throughout this period, debate continued over the role of 'choice' in American education. As some researchers documented higher achieve-ment levels in private schools, particularly the Catholic school system, policymakers renewed their fight to enhance parental choice in educa-tion through tuition voucher programs.

Focus on Excellence

The education reform movement of the 1980s arose out of a growing concern about the quality and effectiveness of public education in the United States. This concern was fueled by the publication of over a dozen reports in 1983 and 1984 that sounded a common theme: the American educational system was in trouble. *A Nation at Risk*, a report of the National Commission on Excellence in Education, issued the strongest indictment of the system: the *average graduate* of the country's schools and colleges in the early 1980s was not as well-educated as 'the average graduate of 25 or 35 years ago, when a much smaller proportion of our population completed high school and college'.[2] All of the studies concluded that students in the United States were not receiving the type of education necessary to meet the demands of a technological society or to maintain the nation's competitive economic position internationally.

These reports presented two kinds of evidence as proof of the scope and seriousness of the educational problem: declining test scores during the late 1960s and 1970s and the relatively poor performance of American students on international assessments.

Declining test scores

The most frequently cited indicator of the failings of the public school system was the score decline on the College Board's Scholastic Aptitude Tests (SAT). The SAT has been used by colleges and universities since the 1920s as one measure of high school students' preparedness for postsecondary education. The test includes verbal and mathematical sections. Scores are reported separately for each section on a scale of 200 to 800. Between 1963 and 1977, average verbal scores fell nearly 50 points (from 478 to 429) and average mathematics scores dropped 32 points (from 502 to 470).[3] Concern about this decline led to the appointment of a blue-ribbon panel by the College Board and Educational Testing Service (ETS) in the mid-1970s to investigate the causes of the decline. The Panel concluded that the decline had occurred in two distinct stages, with each characterized by a different set of causal factors.

The first stage of the SAT score decline, between 1963 and 1970, resulted in large part from a drastic change in the composition of the SAT-taking population. The SAT was originally limited to a relatively small segment of the high school population headed for elite private colleges, largely in the eastern portion of the country. In the 1960s, however, the test-taking population expanded to include students attending less selective four year colleges, two-year colleges and training programs with more technical and vocational emphasis. Larger proportions of the new test-takers came from three groups that have tended toward lower scores: students from low socioeconomic status families, members of minority groups, and (on the mathematics test) women.

There were relatively small changes in the number and characteristics of students taking the SAT between 1970 and 1977. Yet, the score decline continued through this period and it was pervasive — that is, it showed up within virtually all categories of SAT takers. After considering approximately 50 hypotheses, the panel members concluded that 'there is no *one* cause of the SAT score decline, at least as far as we can discern, and we suspect no single pattern of causes'.[4] The panel did identify six developments, however, that may have contributed to falling scores:

1. the proliferation of elective courses;
2. the lowering of academic standards in both high school and college;
3. the competition of television;
4. the weakening of the role of the family in the educational process;
5. national tensions; and
6. diminution of students' learning motivation.

Successive national assessments of the general student population throughout the 1970s also showed a steady decline in certain achievement areas. The National Assessment of Educational Progress (NAEP) tests a representative sample of the national population of 9, 13 and 17-year-olds. In contrast to the SAT, the first three reading assessments conducted by the NAEP between 1970–71 and 1979–80 showed no substantial overall decline in the achievement of 17-year-olds. A decline was apparent, however, in the 17-year-olds performance on higher order reading skills, such as inferential comprehension which requires the student to draw inferences from the material explicitly stated in the question.[5] A modest decline in mathematics achievement occurred between 1972 and 1977 for the 17-year-old population. The decline was especially severe in the areas of the problem-solving and the application of mathematics.[6]

International comparisons

A second area of concern, particularly in the business community, was the relatively poor educational preparation of American students compared to students in other countries. At a time when colleges and universities in the United States were reducing the amount of mathematics and science required for admission, Japanese secondary schools were requiring college-bound students to take three natural science courses and four mathematics courses during a three-year program. High school students in the Soviet Union were taking five years of compulsory physics courses and four years of chemistry, while only 21 per cent of American high school students took one or more years of physics and 38 per cent took one or more years of chemistry.[7]

The impact of this differential preparation was seen in the preliminary results of the Second International Mathematics Study and the Second International Science Study. The mathematics assessment showed the US eighth graders ranked at about the average of fourteen countries, but twelfth graders fell well below the international average. Japanese students ranked at the top in each grade tested. The science study found that students in England, Japan and six other un-named countries out-performed the top American students — those who were taking advanced courses in physics, chemistry and biology.

The National Commission on Excellence in Education and several of the other study commissions identified five general causes of these deficiencies in educational performance: (i) changing demographics and societal values which had changed the role of the schools; (ii) lower expectations for students; (iii) a less rigorous educational program; (iv) insufficient time spent on school work; and (v) inadequately prepared teachers. A series of recommendations emerged from this diagnosis. These recommendations addressed school curriculum, programs for special populations, college entrance requirements, performance standards for students, training of teachers, administrative leadership, fiscal support, and the proper role of local, state and federal governments in strengthening the educational process.

The studies generated an unexpected response from the press, the public and the President. Throwing his support behind the work of the National Commission on Excellence in Education, President Reagan toured the country speaking about the need to reform the national education system. Governors, state boards of education and state legislatures established nearly 300 state-level study commissions, proposed countless education reform measures, and adopted many of the recommendations contained in the national reports. Forty-one states responded by raising course work standards for high school graduation, 22 states implemented or expanded their minimum competency testing programs and many states began to test aspiring teachers.[8]

Focus on Equity

The reports and the subsequent flurry of state activity were quickly criticized on the grounds that they addressed only the needs of the 'top

50 per cent' of high school students. Groups such as the Children's Defense Fund and the National Coalition of Advocates for Students argued that in the rush to bring excellence to schools by raising academic standards, policymakers ignored the needs of the nation's 'at risk' students. They defined 'at risk' children as those 'who happen to be born different by virtue of race, language, sex, or income status'.[9] These are the children who are the most likely to receive only minimal educational opportunities, the most likely to show lower test scores and the most likely to drop out of high school.

While the major reports recognized in general terms that these students have special needs, they failed to discuss how schools can educate students who do not come from homes with middle-class values and middle-class incomes. In fact, it was argued that reforms that create higher standards, without changing the way that we educate disadvantaged students, will force more students out of school.[10]

Two trends have made state policymakers increasingly receptive to the concerns of the child advocacy groups. First, the proportion of school children coming from families who are poor, minority and/or are not proficient in English is growing. Between 1970 and 1980, the percentage of minority public school children increased from 21 to 27 per cent. One-third of the children entering school in the late 1980s will be nonwhite. In addition, nearly one-quarter of these new students will come from families with incomes below the poverty line and nearly one-half of them will be raised by a single parent during some period before they turn eighteen.[11]

Second, the disparity in achievement between racial/ethnic groups, particularly Black and White students, has not narrowed over time. The first definitive quantification of these differences was reported in 1966. Analyzing data from the Congressionally-mandated Equality of Educational Opportunity Study, Coleman and his colleagues found that with some exceptions (notably Asian Americans), the achievement of the average minority student was distinctly lower than the achievement of the average White student at every grade level. The difference persisted across grades, as well. For example, Black students in the metropolitan Northeast scored about 1.1 standard deviations below Whites in the same region at grades 6, 9 and 12.[12]

This gap has remained in spite of improvements in performance by Blacks and Hispanics during the 1970s and early 1980s. Data from NAEP show that improvements in reading proficiency between 1971 and 1984 were greatest for those groups that were furthest behind in 1971 — Black and Hispanic students. For example, the percentage of

Black 9-year-olds who had not acquired rudimentary reading skills and strategies was cut in half during this period, while the proportion of Black 17-year-olds with adept reading skills and strategies more than doubled. Yet, by 1984, White 17-year-olds were nearly three times as likely to have mastered adept reading skills as Black and Hispanic students at this age. Put another way, the average proficiency levels of Black and Hispanic 17-year-olds on the NAEP reading assessment were only slightly greater than those for White 13-year-olds.[13]

SAT scores for Black and Hispanics also improved relative to Whites during the later 1970s and early 1980s.[14] Yet, in 1982, the average verbal and mathematics scores for Black and Mexican American SAT takers were, respectively, one standard deviation and two-thirds of a standard deviation lower than the average scores for White test-takers.[15]

Focus on Choice

The existence of non-public schools has always lent an element of diversity to American education. The right of parental choice in education has resulted in a private high school population of about 10 per cent. Nearly three-quarters of these students attend Catholic parochial schools, and for decades churchmen and parents of parochial school children have sought to secure public funds for their schools. In recent years, this effort has been bolstered by academics and policy-makers who see public support of private elementary and secondary education as a way of fostering competition, diversity and innovation in educational programs and increasing parental involvement in schooling and schools' accountability to parents and the public. Supporters of two proposals for securing public funds for parents of private school students — tuition vouchers and tuition tax credits — point to research that showed that students attending Catholic schools achieve at a higher level than those enrolled in public schools, even after differences in family background are held constant.[16]

Despite a number of highly publicized initiative ballot campaigns and debates in Congress and in state legislatures, opponents of voucher plans and tuition tax credits have generally been successful in thwarting their adoption. Supporters of public schools argue that these mechanisms would lead to unfair competition, in which non-selective public schools, enrolling children of the poor and of racial minorities, and the handicapped, would be at a disadvantage compared with selective private schools, which can screen out 'undesirable' or troublesome applicants. In addition, given the perilous state of financial support for schools in many areas of the nation (and particularly in many urban centers where private schools are most prevalent), public schools argue that they cannot accept a diversion of funds to non-public education.

In the last few years, however, states and school districts have taken action to increase parental choice *within* the public school system. Magnet schools have become a powerful tool in achieving racial integration in urban school systems. Cambridge, Massachusetts and the predominantly Hispanic East Harlem community school district in New York City provide an elaborate system of choice options to parents of public school children within their boundaries. 'Second chance' options, which permit certain categories of 'at risk' students to attend a program of their choice in another school or school district already exists in several states. The National Governors' Association has called on states to expand this concept by permitting families to enroll their children in other public school systems within a state.

Summary

Education policymaking in the 1980s in the United States, as in earlier decades, reflects ongoing tensions between the values of excellence, equity and choice. Declining test scores, both within the country and relative to the performance of students abroad, triggered a call for higher standards in curriculum, teaching and student achievement. Concern about the impact of higher standards on 'at risk' students, and a continued disparity in the tested achievement of Whites and many minority group students, has made policymakers sensitive to the need to change the way that disadvantaged students are educated. A growing question, however, is whether the public sector can do the best job of educating all students, or whether public funds should support alternative education programs and enhance parental choice among competing educational programs.

Determinants of Achievement

The challenge to educators, policymakers, parents and citizens as the nation enters the decade of the 1990s, therefore, is to provide a quality education to an increasingly diverse student population. Meeting that challenge, however, requires a greater understanding of what school processes and school-related behaviors are associated with higher achievement for different groups of learners. The commission reports said little about these relationships. The information they presented was 'patchy and dated', with few references to recent literature and research dealing with schools.[17]

The design of our study draws on nearly twenty-five years of research by sociologists, economists, social psychologists and educational researchers that has examined the relationship between school and student characteristics and educational outcomes. The work has been characterized by an on-going debate over the relative influence of four groups of variables — student demographics, the home educational support system, student school experiences, and school resources and processes — on student achievement. We use these four categories to summarize this body of research.

Student Demographics

The influence of social factors on academic achievement was one of the earliest subjects in education to come under controlled study by researchers.[18] The first large-scale analysis of this relationship was conducted as part of the Equality of Educational Opportunity (EED) study. The authors found that family background accounted for a substantial amount of school-to-school variation in tested achievement; variations in school facilities, curriculum and staff had only a small independent effect on academic performance. When family background characteristics were statistically controlled for, the social composition of the school's student body and students' attitudes and values explained more of the variance in achievement than any school factor.

These findings challenged widely held assumptions about the way schools affect learning. One interpretation of the conclusions held that 'schools do not make a difference'. Those accepting this view believed that public schools do not, and cannot, ensure equality of educational opportunity; they merely perpetuate the inequalities between children that accrue from differences in their family backgrounds.

Nearly every major study conducted since that time has, like Coleman, showed a positive relationship between students' background characteristics and measures of school performance. The studies have differed, however, in the particular inputs that were used to define student background. In the EEO analysis, student's individual characteristics included race/ethnicity and students' interest in school, self-concept, and locus of control. Coleman concluded in that study that attitudes such as sense of control of the environment or a belief in the responsiveness of the environment, as well as demographic characteristics, were highly related to achievement. In fact, Black students who had a strong sense of control of environment did better than White students with a weak sense. These findings were supported in more disaggregated analyses of the EEO data by Mayeske *et al.*,[19] and by studies involving other data bases. The more students feel a sense of control over the environment (i.e., internally-oriented), the better their self-concept, or the higher their academic motivation, the higher their levels of tested verbal achievement.[20]

In a review of subsequent input-output studies, Bridge, Judd and Moock[21] categorized individual student inputs as students' sex, preschool experiences, age, affective inputs and school attendance. A review of selected literature on associations between education outcomes and background variables prepared by Bryant, Glaser, Hansen and Kirsch[22] for NAEP focused on different measures of socioeconomic status and on characteristics of the student that they considered to be 'immutable' — race, sex, age, family structure and student ability.

Our study includes three sets of student background variables: (i) student demographics; (ii) family characteristics; and (iii) students' aspirations, attitudes and values. We use five measures of student demographics: (i) sex; (ii) socioeconomic status; (iii) race/ethnicity; (iv) geographic region; and (v) community type. Socioeconomic status is an equally weighted composite consisting of father's occupation, family income and number of selected household items. Self-reports were used to group students into seven racial/ethnic groups: White, non-Hispanic; Black; Asian American; American Indian; Mexican American; Puerto Rican and Other Hispanic. In some analyses, Mexican Americans, Puerto Ricans and Other Hispanics were combined into a 'Hispanic' category. Students are also grouped into four geographic regions (Northeast, North Central, South and West) and community type (urban, suburban and rural). Family characteristics include parental education and employment and family structure. Students' aspirations, attitudes and values are measured by self-reports of educational and occupational aspirations, educational plans after high school, self-esteem and locus of control.

Home Educational Support System

Research has shown that family background also has a major impact on student achievement. Again, studies differ as to the variables included as family background characteristics. For example, some researchers treat socioeconomic status as a family variable, rather than a student background characteristic. Others separate economic variables from those family variables that appear to be more directly supportive of students' educational aspirations and activities.

We include three variables in our definition of the home educational support system: (i) number of study aids in the home; (ii) mother's educational aspiration for the student; and (iii) students' exposure to non-school learning experiences, such as music and dancing lessons, travel, and trips to museums.

Student School Experiences

Certain student school experiences, as well as background characteristics and attitudes, have been found to influence achievement. These experiences include study habits, amount of homework completed, number and type of courses taken, television-watching habits, and behavior (or misbehavior) in school. Several studies have reported a positive relationship between the number of courses taken in high school and performance on a number of different types of tests: the SAT, the ACT and tests included in the NLS survey.[23] This relationship was more apparent for areas in which learning is most closely linked to school course work (e.g., mathematics or science). Still others have linked time spent on homework with grades. Keith, for example, found a significant relationship between time spent studying and grades in high school even when race, family background, student ability and field of study are controlled.[24]

We include the following set of student experiences in our analyses: curricular track in high school, time spent on homework, participation in extracurricular activities, and the number, type and level of courses taken in high school.

School Characteristics

Much of the research conducted since the publication of Coleman's EEO study in 1966 has focused, at least in part, on addressing the questions: Do schools make a difference? What things that seem alterable by policymakers have the greatest influence on student achievement? The studies, which use a variety of methodologies and data bases, fall into three general categories: (i) the use of large-scale survey research to identify and measure the independent contribution of school processes on variations in either individual student achievement or average achievement for a school; (ii) the use of descriptive ethnographic and case studies designed to explore and explain the effects of school organization on the processes of teaching and learning that influence student outcomes; and (iii) the use of large-scale data bases to explore the differential impact of school sector (e.g., public, parochial and private) on student outcomes.

Research during the late 1960s and the 1970s concentrated on allocating the variance in educational outcomes between institutional and individual characteristics in an effort to isolate or to estimate the degree to which school resources and facilities affect academic outcomes. Studies using this basic approach appeared in several disciplines. Sociologists concentrated on school climate or context; economists used input-output and production-function models. Common to both disciplines, however, was the use of large-scale survey research and the finding that it was difficult to disentangle the influences of student and family backgrounds and the influences of school facilities, curriculum and staff. For example, using the individual student as the basic unit of analysis, Mayeske *et al.*, found that the independent role of school-related variables on achievement was only about 4 per cent. They hypothesized that the joint effects of family and school inputs could be explained by the tendency of students of similar family background to attend school together and for the achievement mix of entering students to set a 'going rate' that, once established, affects each student independent of family background.[25] Subsequent analyses of the High School and Beyond data concluded that school variables accounted for only 6 to 7 per cent of variation in test scores of high school seniors.[26]

These kinds of studies were criticized, however, as treating schooling as a 'black box' phenomenon. By focusing on the relatively narrow range of institutional variation observed between schools, by looking only at the uniform impact of specific schools on all students, and by using non-experimental methods to deduce causal factors, these analyses of school effects could not effectively identify the characteristics of schools that promote student achievement generally and could not address the question of what sorts of schools were best for what sorts of students. In an effort to overcome these deficiencies, social scientists turned to descriptive ethnographic and case studies designed to explore and explain the effects of school organization on the processes of teaching and learning that influence student outcomes. This 'effective schools' research distinguished explicitly the within-school processes from those operating between schools, and shifted from a macro-institutional to a micro-institutional approach. It yielded a body of empirical literature on the impact of classroom interaction patterns, teachers, principals, tracking, instructional quality and time on task.[27]

The debate over whether schools make a difference changed focus in 1981 when Coleman and his associates released the first major analysis of the 1980 High School and Beyond data.[28] Looking at the differential impact of school sector, they reported that high school seniors in Catholic high schools in 1980 scored higher than their public school counterparts, after controlling for differences in family background. The researchers attributed the better performance of students in Catholic schools to factors related to the more favorable disciplinary climate and quality of instruction in these schools and used these findings to suggest that public policy should encourage an expanded role for private education in the United States.

In a subsequent analysis of the impact of school sector on growth in academic achievement in high school, Coleman and Hoffer argue that differential performance across sectors is also a function of different orientations to schooling.[29] The public school is viewed as an agent of the larger society or the state; its purpose is to 'free the child from constraints imposed by accident of birth'. The Catholic school (and other religious schools) acts as an agent of the community, albeit the religious community. Catholic schools are part of a functional community, representing families with shared values. The private, non-parochial school serves the needs of the individual family, which searches for that school which most closely accords with its values. These orientations, with their different goals, lead to schools with different designs that attract different kinds of families and have different impacts on their students. The authors argue, for example, that it has been the ability of this functional community to withstand the weakening of the high school curriculum and other changes that accompanied the education reforms of the 1960s that explains the stronger educational program in the Catholic high schools.

Our analyses are influenced by these three bodies of research. Our methodology builds on the numerous 'school effects' studies conducted over the last twenty years. The findings of the 'school effectiveness' studies have informed our selection of school characteristics to be included in the relational analyses. Coleman's most recent works (and the controversy surrounding them) led us to consider whether those school processes that are successful in Catholic schools are also successful in the public sector. By asking the broader questions of *which* components of the educational process impact on achievement we treat school sector as only one of the variables in our model.

We include a number of school measures in our analyses. They are grouped into four categories: (i) school sector (public, private); (ii) staff characteristics (e.g., student/teacher ratio, teacher turnover and level of teachers' education); (iii) academic emphasis (number of advanced course offerings, percentage of students who are college-bound and availability of special educational programs); and (iv) student ratings of school quality.

Summary

For nearly twenty-five years, researchers have sought to explain the sources of variation in educational achievement in an attempt to identify practices that would improve our educational system. Some of the variation has been explained by the background characteristics that students bring to school; little of the variation has been explained by differences in the structure and operation of America's schools. In this study, we look at the relative contribution that groups of variables, as well as individual variables, played in changes in tested achievement between 1972 and 1982 and in cognitive growth in the last two years in high school. By examining the differential impact of student demographics, home educational support systems, school processes and student educational experiences, we can assess the extent to which school and schooling processes 'make a difference' in the education of American youth. This approach also enables us to identify those critical variables that can be influenced or changed through education policy.

Overview of Book and Study Methodology

The findings reported in this book are based on analyses of data from two nationally-representative surveys of high school students conducted by the Center for Statistics of the US Department of Education — the National Longitudinal Survey of 1972 (NLS-72), and High School and Beyond (HS&B). These two longitudinal surveys provide a unique data base with which to compare and contrast the nation's high school seniors across the decade 1972 to 1982; to examine the dynamics of cognitive growth and social development in the last two years of high school; and to investigate the influence of student demographics, the home educational support system, student educational experiences and school processes on changes in tested achievement both over time and during the high school years. This section briefly describes the two data bases and summarizes the methodologies we used to analyze change in high school seniors and their schools between 1972 and 1982 and to examine achievement gains of high school students between their sophomore and senior years.

Data Bases

NLS-72 is an ongoing survey that focuses on the educational, vocational and personal development of a representative sample of students who were high school seniors in 1972, and on the personal, familial, social, institutional and cultural factors that directly or indirectly influence that development. The study began in 1972 when over 16,000 seniors in more than 1,000 public and private high schools took a battery of tests and completed questionnaires about themselves and their plans for the future. These students were selected through a two-stage probability sample, with schools as the first stage units and students within schools as the second stage units. With the exception of special strata, schools were selected with probability proportional to estimated enrollment, and within each school, seniors were randomly selected. Schools in low income areas or with high percentages of minority-group students were over-sampled.[30]

Students were tested in reading, vocabulary and mathematics. They were also asked to complete a questionnaire that covered their high school experiences, attitudes, plans for the future and demographic information. A school questionnaire collected information about each school's programs, resources and grading system.

In 1980, NCES launched its second longitudinal study, High School and Beyond. Base-year data were collected that year from approximately 30,000 sophomores in over 1,015 public and private high schools. Once again, a two-stage probability sample was used to select students, and over-sampling was done for special strata schools, including schools that were predominately Hispanic, Catholic schools that had substantial Black enrollments, alternative schools, high performance private schools, and other non-Catholic private schools.

The test battery was expanded to include tests in science, writing and civics, as well as reading, vocabulary and mathematics. The reading and vocabulary tests were essentially the same as the 1972 tests; the mathematics test was similar but expanded. Student and school questionnaires, which contained a number of items comparable or similar to the 1972 questionnaires, were completed by the students and school administrators.[31] Two years later (spring 1982), a follow-up survey collected data from and retested over 22,000 of these students who were seniors in 1982 and over 2,000 individuals who had dropped out of school by 1982. School administrators completed a relatively comparable school questionnaire as well.

Methodology

Part 2 of this book describes changes in American high schools and their students between 1972 and 1982 and relates these changes to the test score declines of the same period. We use descriptive analyses to document changes in student background characteristics and attitudes, family educational support, student educational experiences and the schools. This provides a subset of critical input and process variables for use in relating changes in test scores to changes in student demographics and school processes. Changes in family background variables and student attitudes, behaviors and educational experiences are related to five student background characteristics: (i) sex, (ii) socio-economic status, (iii) race/ethnicity, (iv) region of the country in which they reside, and (v) the type of community in which they reside. Changes in school processes are grouped by four kinds of school characteristics: (i) school sector or type (public, Catholic and private non-parochial); (ii) average socioeconomic status of the student body; (iii) type of community in which the school is located; and (iv) the region of the country.

In order to measure changes in the tested achievement of high school seniors in 1972 and 1982, we used item response theory (IRT) to equate tests across the two populations. Mathematics, vocabulary and reading scores were put on the 1972 score scale.[32] Differences between the 1982 and 1972 test score means are shown in the formula-corrected number-right true score metric and by effect size. The formula-corrected number-right true score are on the same scale as the formula-corrected raw scores and thus can be interpreted in the same way. Effect size is the difference between means divided by the pooled standard deviation. Because effect size is scaled in terms of standard deviation units, and since it is independent of sample size, it allows one to make rough comparisons of the relative magnitude of changes across populations and/or in outcome variables having different metrics.

In addition to identifying changes in student behaviors and tested achievement, we sought to determine the extent to which changes in test scores were related to changes in student, family and school characteristics. We first used a 'population shift' partition of mean test score changes in order to determine how much of the test score decline was due to changes in the demographic characteristics of the students, how much was due to changes in the average test score of different groups of students, and how much was due to an interaction between the two. A 'step down' analysis of covariance was than used to estimate how 1972–1982 changes in school characteristics, as well as changes in population demographics, student behavior and home educational support systems separately affected the average score decline.

Part 3 of this book focuses on the behaviors and tested achievement of high school students during their last two years in (or out of) high school. Path analyses were used to identify those factors that impacted achievement gains of students who completed high school. The model, which is described in detail in Chapter 6, relates student demographics, family educational support system and student behaviors (in and out of school) to gains in tested achievement. Its primary goal is to estimate the effect of relatively manipulable student school behaviors on sophomore to senior year gains independent of demographic and sophomore achievement inputs. The model contrasts Whites with selected racial/ethnic minority groups to identify possible level differences in their home educational support system and student behaviors. In addition, it was run separately within racial/ethnic group to determine whether the educational process works the same way for racial/ethnic minority groups as for White students.

Finally, two kinds of analyses were conducted to examine the question: who drops out of high school and why? Descriptive analysis was used to describe who stayed in school and who dropped out between the sophomore and senior years. Students who stayed in school ('stayers') were compared with those who did not complete school ('dropouts') on a number of dimensions: race/ethnicity, socio-economic status, family structure, home educational support system, ability and attitudes and school behaviors. Path analysis was then used to identify which factors tended to be related to a student's decision to stay in or drop out of school. In addition, we conducted a value-added analysis to estimate the relative impact of staying in or dropping out of school on gains in tested achievement.

Part 4 concludes the book with a summary of our findings and a discussion of the implications of these findings for the development of future educational policy.

Notes and References

1. JAMES, T. and TYACK, D. (1983) 'Learning from past efforts to reform the high school', *Phi Delta Kappan*, February, pp. 400–6.
2. NATIONAL COMMISSION ON EXCELLENCE IN EDUCATION (1983) *A Nation at Risk: The Imperative for Educational Reform* Washington, DC, US Department of Education.
3. ADVISORY PANEL ON THE SCHOLASTIC APTITUDE TEST SCORE DECLINE (1977) *On Further Examination*, New York, College Entrance Examination Board.
4. *Ibid.*, p. 48.
5. NATIONAL ASSESSMENT OF EDUCATIONAL PROGRESS (1981) *Three National Assessments of Reading*, Denver, NAEP/Education Commission of the States.
6. NATIONAL ASSESSMENT OF EDUCATIONAL PROGRESS (1979) *Changes in Mathematical Achievement, 1973–1978*, Denver, NAEP/Education Commission of the States.
7. Fact sheets prepared for the NATIONAL TASK FORCE ON EDUCATION FOR ECONOMIC GROWTH (1982) *Education for a High Technology Economy*. Materials prepared for governors' special briefings. Denver, Education Commission of the States.
8. GOERTZ, M. E. (1986) *State Educational Standards: A 50-State Survey*, Princeton, NJ, Educational Testing Service, RR-86-2.
9. *Barriers to Excellence: Our Children at Risk* (1985), A report of the National Coalition of Advocates for Students National Board of Inquiry (H. Howe II and M. W. Edelman, co-chairpersons), Boston, National Coalition of Advocates for Students.
10. *Ibid.*; LEVIN, H. M. (1985) *The Educationally Disadvantaged: A National Crisis*, The State Youth Initiatives Project, Working Paper #6, Philadelphia, Public/Private Ventures.
11. HODGKINSON, H. L. (1986) 'Reform? Higher education? Don't be absurd!', *Phi Delta Kappan* 68, 4, pp. 271–274.
12. COLEMAN, J. S. *et al.* (1966) *Equality of Educational Opportunity*, Washington, DC, Office of Education, US Department of Health, Education and Welfare, US Government Printing Office.
13. NATIONAL ASSESSMENT OF EDUCATIONAL PROGRESS (1985) *The Reading Report Card: Progress Toward Excellence in Our Schools. Trends in Reading over Four National Assessments, 1971–1984*, Princeton, NJ, NAEP/Educational Testing Service.
14. ETS BOARD OF TRUSTEES (1984) *1984 Public Accountability Report*, Princeton, NJ, Educational Testing Service.

15. RAMIST, L. and ARBEITER, S. (1984) *Profiles, College-Bound Seniors, 1982,* New York, College Entrance Examination Board.
16. COLEMAN, J. S., HOFFER, T. and KILGORE, S. (1982) *High School Achievement: Public, Catholic and Private Schools Compared,* New York, Basic Books.
17. See for example, PETERSON, P. E. (1983) 'Did the Education Commissions say anything?' *The Brookings Review,* Winter, pp. 3–11; and EDELL FELT, R. A. (1984) 'Policy questions prompted by seven recent reports on education'. Unpublished report submitted to the US Department of Education, National Institute of Education under Contract No. NIE-P-83-0091.
18. ROSSI, P. H., 'Social factors in academic achievement: A brief review' as cited in MOSTELLER, F. and MOYNIHAN, D. P. (1972) 'A pathbreaking report: Further studies of the Coleman report' in MOSTELLER, F. and MOYNIHAN, D. P. (Eds) *On Equality of Educational Opportunity,* New York, Vintage Books.
19. MAYESKE, G. W. *et al.,* (1973) *A Study of the Achievement of Our Nation's Students,* Washington, DC, US Department of Health, Education and Welfare, Office of Education, DHEW OE 72–131.
20. BRIDGE, R. G., JUDD, C. M. and MOOCK, P. R. (1979) *The Determinants of Educational Outcomes: The Impact of Families, Peers, Teachers and Schools,* Cambridge, MA, Ballinger Publishing Company, pp. 205–6.
21. *Ibid.*
22. BRYANT, E. C., GLASER, E., HANSEN, M. H. and KIRSCH, A. (1974) *Associations between Educational Outcomes and Background Variables: A Review of Selected Literature,* Denver, NAEP/Education Commission of the States.
23. See for example, SCHMIDT, W. H. (1983) 'High school course-taking: Its relationship to achievement' *Journal of Curriculum Studies,* 15, pp.311–332; ALEXANDER, K. and PALLAS, A. (1984) 'Curriculum reform and school performance: An evaluation of the new basics', *American Journal of Education,* 92, pp. 391–420; and LAING, J., ENGEN, H. MAXEY, J. (1987) 'Relationships between ACT test scores and high school courses', Paper presented at the annual meeting of the Association for Counseling and Development.
24. KEITH, T. K. (1982) 'Time spent on homework and high school grades: A large sample path analysis', *Journal of Educational Psychology,* 74, 2, pp. 248–253.
25. MAYESKE, G. W., *et al.* (1973) *op. cit.*
26. PENG, S. S., OWINGS, J. A., and FETTERS, W. B. (1982) 'Effective high schools: What are their attributes', Paper presented at the annual meeting of the American Psychological Association; and WALBERG, H. J. and SHANAHAN, T. (1983) 'High school effects on individual students', *Educational Researcher* 12, 7, pp. 4–9.
27. See for example, BROOKOVER, W., BEADY, C., FLOOD, P., SCHWEITZER, J. and WISENBAKER, J. (1979) *School Social Systems and Student Achievement: Schools Can Make a Difference,* New York, Praeger; EDMONDS, R. R. (1979) 'Effective schools for the urban poor', *Educational Leadership,* 37, pp. 15–27; EDMONDS, R. R. (1982) 'Programs of school improve-

ment: An overview' *Educational Leadership*, 40, 3, pp. 4–11; MURNANE, R. J. (1980) *Interpreting the Evidence on School Effectiveness*, Working Paper No. 830, New Haven, CT, Institute for Social and Policy Studies, Yale University; and ODDEN, A. and WEBB, L. D. (Eds) (1983) *School Finance and School Improvement Linkages in the 1980s*, Cambridge, MA, Ballinger Publishing Company.

28. COLEMAN, J. S., HOFFER, T. and KILGORE, S. (1982) *High School Achievement: Public, Catholic and Private Schools Compared*, New York, Basic Books.

29. COLEMAN, J. S. and HOFFER, T. (1987) *Public and Private High Schools: The Impact of Communities*, New York, Basic Books.

30. Detailed information about the 1972 sample can be found in RICCO-BONO, J., HENDERSON, L. B., BURKHEIMER, G. J., PLACE, C. and LEVIN-SOHN, J. R. (1981) *National Longitudinal Study: Base Year (1972) through Fourth Follow-up (1979) Data File Users Manual* Research Triangle Park, NC, Research Triangle Institute.

31. Detailed information about the 1980 HS&B sample can be found in FRANKEL, M. R., KOHNKE, L., BUONANNO, D. and TOURANGEOU, R. (1981) *Sample Design Report* Report to the National Center for Education Statistics by the National Opinion Research Center.

32. Technical information on the equating of the items is found in ROCK, D. A., HILTON, T. L., POLLACK, J., EKSTROM, R. B. and GOERTZ, M. E. (1985) *Psychometric Analysis of the NLS and the High School and Beyond Test Batteries* Washington, DC, National Center for Education Statistics, US Department of Education, NCES 85-218.

PART 2
THE AMERICAN HIGH SCHOOL AND ITS STUDENTS: HOW DID THEY CHANGE BETWEEN 1972 AND 1982?

Introduction

This part is divided into four chapters. The first three chapters describe changes in US high schools and high school seniors between 1972 and 1982. Demographic changes, changes in family characteristics, and changes in students' aspirations, attitudes and values are discussed in Chapter 2. Chapter 3 describes changes in the characteristics of the high schools and Chapter 4 looks at the experiences of students in these high schools at these two points in time, especially those school experiences that may be related to intellectual growth and to learning.

These same factors, demographics, family, school characteristics, and students' school experiences, are then used in Chapter 5 to explore how the changes in students and schools are related to declining test scores. There are two hypotheses about the reasons for declining test scores. One is that these changes are the result of changes in the high school population, especially the shift toward larger numbers of minority students. The other hypothesis is that the test score decline is due primarily to changes in school standards and processes. We will use the NLS-72 and HS&B 1982 senior cohort data to explore the validity of these hypotheses.

2   Changes in the Characteristics of High School Seniors and Their Families Between 1972 and 1982

In 1972 the United States was in the midst of the Vietnam War. Richard Nixon was completing his first term as president. Events associated with the 1972 presidential election campaign — especially the Watergate break-in and its aftermath — are still remembered by most adults in the United States. Fewer probably remember that 1972 was the first presidential election in which eighteen year-olds were eligible to vote. Many citizens of other countries, as well as those of the United States, can recall the terrorism at the 1972 Olympic Games in Munich, Germany that resulted in the death of eleven Israeli athletes. This was also the year that the United States Congress passed the Equal Rights Amendment to the Constitution, providing women equal treatment under the law, and sent it to the states for ratification.

On the educational scene, school populations were continuing to grow. Over 15 million students were enrolled in secondary education (grades 9–12). Only a year earlier the Supreme Court had ruled that bussing of students could be ordered to achieve racial desegregation; as a consequence, many schools were in the process of implementing desegregation programs. Title IX of the Education Amendments of 1972 prohibited discrimination in education on the basis of sex; this provided young women with greater access to educational programs and extra-curricular activities. Test scores of college-bound students on the Scholastic Aptitude Test (SAT) stood at 453 on the verbal portion of the test and 484 on the mathematical portion. These test scores were beginning a sharp decline. This decline would continue in the decade to come and would become the focus of considerable public concern.

By 1982 many political, economic and educational changes had taken place. The Vietnam War had ended. Ronald Reagan was in the midst of his first term as president of the United States. The United

States, along with much of the rest of the world, was experiencing a severe recession. The unemployment rate in the United States reached its highest level since 1940, standing at 10.8 per cent in November 1982. Over 11 million were unemployed. Moreover, the unemployment rates for youths, especially minority youths, had skyrocketed. For example, the 1982 White youth unemployment rate was about 20 per cent but the unemployment rate for Black youths stood at 46 per cent. The Equal Rights Amendment, passed by Congress in 1972 and intended to remove all legal obstacles for equal treatment of women, had failed to receive ratification by a majority of states in the intervening decade and, therefore, went down to defeat.

There were changes on the educational scene also. The Senate voted for a bill that essentially eliminated bussing for racial integration in schools. Both high school enrollments and test scores had plummeted. Scores on the verbal portion of the Scholastic Aptitude Test, after bottoming out at 424 for two years, rose to 426; mathematics scores also showed a slight rise. These changes prompted many educators to predict a turn-around in the much-discussed test score decline.

High school enrollment in the fall of 1982 stood at approximately 12.5 million, down over 2.5 million from a decade earlier. School enrollment changes varied considerably, however, across areas as people left the Northern region of the country for the 'Sun Belt'. For example, high school enrollments doubled in Nevada and increased by more than a third in Arizona, while, at the same time, North and South Dakota experienced enrollment declines of approximately 25 per cent.

Students and their schools changed as well in the decade of the 1970s. In this chapter we explore the changes in high school seniors' backgrounds and families, and in those attitudes, values, and aspirations that are formed primarily by family and the larger society.

Demographics

The major demographic change in United States high schools between 1972 and 1982 was the increase in minority students. In 1972 approximately 86 per cent of high school seniors were white and 14 per cent minority. By 1982 the proportion of whites had dropped to 77 per cent while the minority proportion rose to 23 per cent (See Table 1). Blacks were 8.5 per cent of all high school seniors in 1972 and nearly 13 per cent in 1982. Hispanics (including Mexican Amer-

Table 1   Demographic changes in high school seniors 1972 to 1982
(Percentages based on weighted data)

	1972	*1982*
	%	%
Sex		
Male	49.9	50.0
Female	50.1	50.0
SES[1]		
Low	24.3	24.4
Middle	51.2	49.9
High	24.4	25.7
Race/Ethnicity		
White	86.1	77.0
Black	8.5	12.9
Mexican American	2.5	4.0
Puerto Rican	0.3	1.1
Other Hispanic	0.6	2.6
Asian American	0.9	1.4
American Indian	1.1	1.0
Geographic Region[2]		
Northeast	27.2	23.6
North Central	29.1	28.5
South	27.0	32.0
West	16.7	16.0
Community Type[3]		
Urban	25.1	20.0
Suburban	53.0	48.8
Rural	21.9	31.2

Notes
1. Socioeconomic status (SES) is a composite variable, assigned on the basis of father's occupation, father's and mother's education, family income, and the availability of certain items in the household. Each of the five components is standardized separately and the components are then averaged to form the raw SES score. This is then divided into quartiles. In this and the other tables in this book, low SES is the lowest quartile, middle SES the two middle quartiles, and high SES the highest quartile. Thus, the socioeconomic level of the two populations cannot be compared.
2. The four regions were defined as follows:
   Northeast — New England and Middle Atlantic states
   Northcentral — East North Central and West North Central states
   South — South Atlantic, East South Central, and West South Central states
   West — Mountain and Pacific states
3. Rural was defined as a rural or farming community; Suburban was defined as a small city or town (50,000 people or less), or as the suburb of a medium, large or very large city; Urban was defined as a medium-sized (50,000–100,000 people), large (100,000–500,000 people) or very large (over 500,000 people) city. This information was collected from students in 1972 and from school administrators in 1982.

icans, Puerto Ricans, and other Hispanic subpopulations) were approximately 3 per cent of all high school seniors in 1972 and nearly 8 per cent of the seniors in 1982.

In the NLS-72 and HS&B data bases, socioeconomic status was assigned to each group of students based on parental education, occupation, and other characteristics. The top quartile was considered to have high socioeconomic status, the lowest quartile to have low socioeconomic status, and the remaining two quartiles to have middle socioeconomic status. This assignment process, unfortunately, makes it impossible to compare family socioeconomic status across the decade.

As indicated earlier, there were also changes in where students lived. As can be seen in Table 1, the percentage of high school seniors residing in Southern states increased by five percentage points; the percentage residing the Northeastern and Northcentral regions decreased by a similar amount. There was also a significant shift of seniors to those communities classified as rural. However, changes in data collection procedures may have resulted in some noncomparability of these categories.

Family Characteristics

The questionnaires used in NLS-72 and HS&B provide information about the occupational and educational background of the students' parents, about these parents' educational aspirations for their children, and about home support for learning.

Parental Education and Employment

The average educational level of the seniors' parents rose slightly between 1972 and 1982. In 1972 the typical parent had completed high school and obtained some post-secondary education, but not a college degree. Mothers averaged somewhat less education than fathers. Parental education varied considerably by SES, with low SES parents typically having less than a high school education and middle SES parents typically having a high school diploma but no college experience.

By 1982 the parents of the typical high school senior had more education than had been the case in 1972, but this was still equivalent to completing high school and having some additional postsecondary education. The rise in parental education was especially noteworthy among parents of minority students and parents of students in non-public schools, but was statistically significant for all segments of the population. Stark contrasts remained across socioeconomic groups, however. In 1982 the male parent of the typical high SES high school senior was a college graduate, while neither parent of the typical low SES student had completed high school.

The parents of the 1972 seniors were employed in a wide range of occupations. Five major occupational groups dominated the work reported for the seniors' fathers. These were craftwork (such as auto mechanic, baker, carpenter, machinist, or plumber) engaged in by 18 per cent; professional work (such as dentist, engineer, nurse, or teacher) 14 per cent; managerial work (such as sales manager, officer manager, buyer, or restaurant manager) 14 per cent; operative work (such as assembler, machine operator, welder, or truck driver) 12 per cent; and laborer (such as assembler, car washer, or sanitary worker) 11 per cent. The mothers' work was less diversified. Approximately 55 per cent were described by their children as full-time homemakers, 16 per cent were reported to do clerical work (such as bank teller, bookkeeper, or secretary), and 9 per cent were described as doing professional work. Not surprisingly, the type of occupation pursued by these parents varied across SES and racial/ethnic lines. For example, the largest proportion of low SES mothers was employed in service occupations, while the middle SES mothers predominated in clerical occupations, and high SES mothers in professional occupations.

Parental occupations shifted slightly between 1972 and 1982, although a slight change in the phrasing of this question (from 'current occupation' to 'current or most recent occupation') makes exact comparisons impossible. Fewer fathers appeared to be employed as laborers (down from 11 per cent to 9 per cent) or as craftsmen (down from 18 per cent to 15 per cent), while more were apparently employed as managers (up from 14 per cent to 16 per cent). Fewer mothers appeared to be primarily homemakers (a drop from 55 per cent to 17 per cent). More mothers seemed to be involved in clerical work (up from 16 per cent to 26 per cent), service work (up from 6 per cent to 14 per cent), and professional work (up from 9 per cent to 16 per cent).

Parents' Educational Aspirations for Their Children

In both 1972 and 1982, students were asked about their parents' educational aspirations for them. (There was a slight change in this question between 1972, when students were asked how much education their mother wanted them to get, and 1982, when students were asked how much education their parents wanted them to get.) The results (a mean response of 3.63 in 1972 and a mean response of 3.74 in 1982) indicate that, in both years, the typical parent wanted his or her child to obtain some college education but not necessarily to graduate from a four-year college. However, the small numerical increase indicates a statistically significant rise in parents' aspirations for their children.

There were variations in these rising aspirations. Parents' educational aspirations for daughters rose significantly, but there was no comparable increase for sons. In 1972 parents' educational aspirations were slightly lower for females (3.51) than for males (3.75), but this reversed by 1982, with a mean of 3.76 for females, 3.71 for males. Parental aspirations for their children increased significantly in middle and upper socioeconomic status families, but not in lower status families. Aspirations were greater for students from high SES families (4.06) than for those from middle (3.55) or low (3.29) SES families but, in each case, college education was the typical goal. Asian American and Black mothers had the highest educational aspirations for their children (4.02 and 3.72, respectively), as contrasted with 3.63 for mothers of White students.

Home Support for Learning

In a surprising contrast to these rising aspirations, there was a small decline in home support for learning across this decade.

To obtain some sense of home support for learning, the students were asked to indicate whether or not certain study aids (e.g., a specific place to study, a daily newspaper, an encyclopedia and/or other reference books, and a typewriter) were available to them at home. Between 1972 and 1982, there was a small but statistically significant decline in the availability of these study aids. In 1972 the typical student reported having an average of slightly more than three (3.21) of these four study aids; by 1982 the typical student reported having 2.97 of these study aids. This decline may be due to a number of factors. One possibility is that it reflects changes in the absolute (rather than the comparative) socioeconomic status of families in the two cohorts. Another possibility is that the relative importance of these and other study aids may have changed in this period. For example, typewriters may have taken on a lesser role and have been replaced, for some students, by a personal computer which would be useful for other learning activities as well as for word processing.

Finally, the change may reflect lower parental concern with providing educational support for their children.

Although the decline in the number of study aids in the home occurred across all socioeconomic levels, regions and community types, the extent of the decline varied considerably. The most noticeable difference is across socioeconomic groups where low SES students, who already averaged fewer study aids in 1972 than their more advantaged classmates, reported the greatest decline; high SES students showed the least decline (See Table 2). By 1982, low SES students averaged only 2.54 study aids, while middle SES students averaged 3.31 and high SES students 3.64. The decline in study aids was somewhat greater for females than for males. There were similar declines for White and Asian American students while Black and Mexican American seniors reported essentially no change in the availability of study aids and Puerto Rican high school seniors reported an increase in the number of study aids in their homes.

One of these study aids appears to us to have considerably more importance than the rest, namely having a place to study. We hypothesize that lack of a typewriter or daily newspaper would have only a minor impact on student achievement. Lack of a place to study, however, would likely reduce students' opportunities to do homework and would, therefore, have a much more direct relationship to student learning. The proportion of high school seniors reporting that they had a place to study declined from 62 per cent in 1972 to 53 per cent in 1982 (See Table 3).

The decline in having a place to study appears to affect almost all groups of students. The decline is greater for females than for males and greater for Whites than for most minority groups. Students from high SES homes were considerably more likely to report having a place to study than low SES students, but we found few differences across racial/ethnic groups.

Students' Aspirations, Attitudes and Values

The questionnaires used in NLS-72 and HS&B provide information about the high school seniors' educational and occupational aspirations, values, and attitudes. Changes in these aspirations, attitudes and values reflect, in large part, changes in their families and in the American society. In turn, these changing aspirations, attitudes and values are likely to affect what students do in school.

Table 2   Mean number of study aids available in homes of high school seniors

	1972	*1982*	*Difference*
Total	3.21	2.97	−0.24*
Sex			
Male	3.19	2.99	−0.21*
Female	3.22	2.95	−0.27*
SES			
Low	2.54	2.22	−0.31*
Middle	3.31	3.07	−0.25*
High	3.64	3.48	−0.16*
Race/Ethnicity	3.28	3.04	−0.24*
White	2.75	2.73	−0.01
Black	2.60	2.60	0.00
Mexican American	2.48	2.70	0.22
Puerto Rican	2.88	2.75	−0.14
Other Hispanic	3.33	3.06	−0.27
Asian American	2.99	2.76	−0.23
American Indian			
Region			
Northeast	3.38	3.09	−0.29*
North Central	3.19	2.98	−0.21*
South	3.05	2.85	−0.20*
West	3.19	3.00	−0.18*
Community Type			
Urban	3.22	2.95	−0.27*
Suburban	3.30	3.06	−0.24*
Rural	2.97	2.84	−0.13

* Difference significant at or beyond .05 level

Students' Educational and Occupational Aspirations

The educational aspirations of high school seniors did not change, on average, between 1972 and 1982. In both years, the students reported the highest level of education they planned to obtain, a point midway between some postsecondary education and the completion of a four-year college (3.42 in 1972 and 3.41 in 1982).

The overall stability of average aspirations masks a number of significant changes in the subgroups (See Table 4). Among the most notable are the variations by gender and by socioeconomic status. In 1972 males had higher educational aspirations than females (3.54 vs. 3.30) and aspirations increased with rising socioeconomic status (from some college for low SES students to completing a four-year college for high SES students). By 1982 we find the educational aspirations of females have risen (3.46) and now surpass the educational aspirations of males (3.37). We also see a further widening of the gap in educational aspirations among students of different socioeconomic status, as higher status students show a significant increase while low and mid-

Table 3 *Percentage of high school seniors having a specific place at home for study*

	1972	1982	Difference
Total	62.3	53.2	−9.0*
Sex			
Male	63.2	55.8	−7.4*
Female	61.4	50.7	−10.7*
SES			
Low	50.4	42.0	−8.4*
Middle	61.7	52.1	−9.6*
High	75.1	65.7	−9.4*
Race/Ethnicity			
White	62.7	52.5	−10.2*
Black	60.2	58.2	−2.0
Mexican American	53.8	51.7	−2.1
Puerto Rican	51.0	52.3	1.2
Other Hispanic	63.9	52.0	−12.0
Asian American	71.5	64.3	−7.2
American Indian	60.1	44.8	−15.4*
Region			
Northeast	67.0	54.1	−12.9*
North Central	58.5	49.5	−9.1*
South	62.2	54.3	−7.9*
West	61.7	56.4	−5.3*
Community Type			
Urban	63.7	55.6	−8.1*
Suburban	64.4	54.8	−9.6*
Rural	54.9	49.2	−5.7*

* Difference significant at or beyond .05 level

dle status students show no significant change in their educational aspirations.

There were no major changes in the educational aspirations of White or Black high school seniors across the 1972 to 1982 decade. Asian American students, who already had higher educational aspirations in 1972 than any other racial/ethnic group, increased their aspirations still further. Mexican American and Puerto Rican students showed a decline in aspirations across the decade.

There is often a gap between high school students' dreams and their immediate plans. Therefore, the students were also asked what they planned to do in the first year after high school (See Table 5). In both 1972 and 1982, approximately a third (34 per cent) of the seniors expected to enter a four-year college directly after high school and about a quarter (25 per cent in 1972, 21 per cent in 1982) expected to enter a two-year college or a postsecondary vocational-technical institution. There was a increase between 1972 and 1982 in seniors planning to work full- or part-time after completing high school (from 28 per cent to 34 per cent).

All of the seniors were asked to indicate the type of work they

Table 4   Mean educational aspirations of high school seniors
(*Scale*: from 1 = not complete high school to 5 = graduate/professional school)

	1972	1982	Difference
Total	3.42	3.41	−0.00
Sex			
Male	3.54	3.37	−0.17*
Female	3.30	3.46	0.16*
SES	2.98	2.93	−0.05
Low	3.32	3.32	−0.01
Middle	3.94	4.04	0.11*
High			
Race/Ethnicity			
White	3.43	3.44	0.01
Black	3.46	3.40	−0.06
Mexican American	3.31	3.04	−0.26*
Puerto Rican	3.47	3.08	−0.38
Other Hispanic	3.28	3.29	0.01
Asian American	3.74	3.98	0.
American Indian	2.90	3.12	0.22
Region			
Northeast	3.43	3.46	0.03
North Central	3.35	3.37	0.02
South	3.45	3.36	−0.09*
West	3.47	3.51	0.04
Community Type			
Urban	3.46	3.44	−0.01
Suburban	3.52	3.51	−0.01
Rural	3.16	3.24	0.09*

* Difference significant at or beyond .05

Table 5   Seniors' plans for the first year after high school

	1972	1982	Difference
	%	%	%
4-Year College	34	34	0
2-Year College/Voc-Tech	25	21	−4
Work, Full- or Part-Time	28	34	6
Other	13	11	−2

wanted to be doing at age 30 (See Table 6). Nearly half (45 per cent of the 1972 seniors and 40 per cent of the 1982 seniors) said they wanted to be in professional work (doctor, lawyer, etc.). The next most popular category in 1972 was clerical work (14 per cent); this declined to 9 per cent by 1982. Interest in technical work rose from 7 per cent to 11 per cent of all seniors, making this the second most popular career category by 1982. Interest in managerial work also rose substantially, from 3 per cent to 8 per cent of all seniors.

Table 6   Work high school seniors would like to do at age 30

	1972	1982
	%	%
Clerical	14	9
Craftsman	8	8
Farmer	2	2
Homemaker	3	3
Laborer	2	2
Manager	3	8
Military	2	3
Operative	2	3
Professional	45	40
Proprietor	2	4
Protective	2	2
Sales	3	2
Service	4	4
Technical	7	11

Students' Belief in Their Academic Ability

The NLS-72 and HS&B questionnaires also included items to assess the seniors' belief in their ability to complete college, their general self-esteem, sense of control over their own destiny (locus of control), career values, and life values. These attitudes and values, which are determined largely by family and the larger society, help us develop a deeper understanding of these young people.

The seniors were asked, regardless of their educational plans, if they thought they had the ability to complete college. Their answers (See Table 7) indicate that, both in 1972 and in 1982, most high school seniors believed they had the intellectual ability to complete college. There was little variation in this belief by sex and among White, Black and Asian American students. However, Hispanic and low socioeconomic status students were less likely than other seniors to believe they had the ability to complete college.

There was a small but statistically significant increase, between 1972 and 1982, in seniors' belief about their ability. This increase occurred in all subgroups except Mexican American students, who showed a small decline. Asian American and American Indian students showed the largest increases in belief they had the ability to complete college. Female students showed a greater increase than males; rural students showed a greater increase than urban and suburban students.

Table 7 Seniors' belief about their ability to complete college
(*Scale*: from 1 = definitely not to 5 = yes, definitely)

	1972	1982	Difference
Total	4.05	4.25	0.20*
Sex			
Male	4.06	4.19	0.14*
Female	4.05	4.30	0.26*
SES			
Low	3.71	3.89	0.18*
Middle	4.03	4.24	0.21*
High	4.45	4.61	0.16*
Race/Ethnicity			
White	4.08	4.27	0.18*
Black	4.04	4.29	0.25*
Mexican American	3.91	3.85	−0.06
Puerto Rican	3.79	4.14	0.35
Other Hispanic	3.95	4.11	0.17
Asian American	4.02	4.47	0 44*
American Indian	3.57	4.13	0.56*
Region			
Northeast	4.08	4.30	0.22*
North Central	3.98	4.21	0.23*
South	4.05	4.20	0.15*
West	4.13	4.33	0.20*
Community Type			
Urban	4.08	4.24	0.16*
Suburban	4.13	4.31	0.18*
Rural	3.87	4.16	0.29*

* Difference significant at or beyond .05 level.

Self-Esteem

The seniors' self-assessment of their academic ability is only one aspect of self-esteem. Four questionnaire items were used to tap other aspects of this variable. These items and the mean ratings given by the seniors are shown in Table 8. As these items show, both the 1972 and the 1982 seniors had a generally positive attitude toward themselves. There were significant increases between 1972 and 1982 toward even more positive self-concept.

Locus of Control

The questionnaires given to the 1972 and 1982 seniors also included four items to determine whether the students felt they had the power to control their own lives (internal locus of control) or felt that life events were beyond their control (external locus of control). The items were scored so that lower numbers indicate an externalized locus of control, or a feeling that one cannot influence what happens in one's life.

The mean scores in both 1972 and 1982 are on the higher (inter-

Table 8   High school seniors' mean ratings on four self-esteem items
(*Scale*: from 1 = disagree strongly to 4 = agree strongly)

Item	1972	1982	Difference
I feel I am a person of worth, on an equal plane with others	3.24	3.33	0.09*
I am able to do things as well as most other people	3.18	3.30	0.12*
I take a positive attitude toward myself	3.13	3.29	0.17*
On the whole, I am satisfied with myself	2.90	3.09	0.19*
Mean for all four items	3.11	3.25	0.14*

* Difference significant at or beyond .05 level.

Table 9   High school seniors' mean ratings on four locus of control items
(*Scale*: from 1 = agree strongly to 4 = disagree strongly)

Item	1972	1982	Difference
Good luck is more important than hard work for success	3.30	3.16	−0.15*
Planning only makes a person unhappy since plans hardly ever work out anyway	3.04	3.04	0.00
Every time I try to get ahead, something or somebody stops me	2.92	2.85	−0.06*
People who accept their condition in life are happier than those who try to change things	2.80	2.66	−0.13*
Mean for all four items	3.01	2.93	−0.08*

* Difference significant at or beyond the .05 level.

nalized) side of the scale midpoint (2.5) indicating that these students feel their behaviors will influence their futures (See Table 9). However the change between 1972 and 1982 was toward externality, suggesting that high school seniors became increasingly less certain, during this decade, that they could control their futures.

Life Values

The students were also asked to rate the importance in their lives of work, family and other activities. The changes in these life values are summarized in Table 10.

In both cohorts, the same five items are rated as having the greatest importance:

- Success in work
- Marriage and family life
- Strong friendships.
- Steady work, and
- Better opportunities for your children.

Table 10   High school seniors' mean ratings of the importance of life values
(*Scale*: from 1 = not significant to 3 = very important)

Item	1972	1982	Difference
Importance in your life of ...			
Success in work	2.83	2.86	0.02*
Marriage and family life	2.77	2.80	0.04*
Strong friendships	2.77	2.78	0.01
Steady work	2.75	2.85	0.10*
Better opportunities for your children	2.60	2.66	0.06*
Working to correct social and economic inequalities	2.06	1.72	−0.34*
Making lots of money	1.95	2.23	0.27*
Being a community leader	1.66	1.58	−0.07*
Living close to parents and relatives	1.57	1.86	0.29*
Getting away from this area	1.57	1.57	−0.01

* Difference significant at or beyond .05 level.

Attitudes about the importance of steady work showed a significant increase between 1972 and 1982 while the other three important life values changed very little across the decade. The greater concern with finding steady work in 1982, as compared with 1972, is not surprising when we remember that the nation was in the midst of a severe recession at that time.

Two of the three other large changes in life values reflect reduced altruism (as indicated by lower interest in correcting social and economic inequities), and a more self-centered desire for financial success (as indicated by the increased interest in making lots of money).

These changes are not surprising; they have been commented on by others studying the American scene. Similar findings have by reported by Astin and his colleagues. A 1986 report from the Cooperative Institutional Research Program[1] states that 'Student endorsement of "being very well-off financially" as a "very important" or "essential" goal in life continued its steady climb to an all-time high of 73.2 per cent this year (up from 70.9 per cent last year and only 39.1 per cent in 1970). Similarly, more freshman than ever before say that a major reason for attending college is "to be able to make more money"' In contrast, virtually all student values having to do with altruism and social concern continued to decline in the 1986 survey.

Today's youth have been described by some as the narcissistic generation. In *The Culture of Narcissism*, Lasch[2] has suggested that narcissism provides us with a way of understanding the psychological impact of recent social changes. Yankelovich[3], while disagreeing with Lasch that narcissism is the essence of the American search for self-fulfillment has, nevertheless, estimated that about 80 per cent of Americans are now committed to this search.

What is surprising, in the values of high school seniors, is the large increase in the importance that 1982 seniors placed on living close to their parents or other relatives. This may be part of a return to more traditional values, especially the importance of the home, or it may be a part of the narcissistic behavior discussed above. Perhaps the 1982 seniors believe that living close to their parents will allow them to continue certain dependent behaviors, rather than living further from home which would require greater self-sufficiency. Alternatively, the greater desire to live close to parents may be linked to the seniors' diminishing sense of control over their lives and, hence, an increased need for parental control and support.

Summary

There were many changes in United States high school seniors' backgrounds, families, aspirations, values and attitudes between 1972 and 1982. The major demographic change was the larger number of minority high school students.

The families of high school seniors showed a number of changes. Parents were somewhat better educated. More mothers worked outside the home. Fewer fathers worked as laborers while a larger percentage were employed in managerial occupations. Parents' educational aspirations for their daughters rose while educational aspirations for sons remained essentially unchanged. Parents' aspirations for their children also increased in middle and upper socioeconomic level families. Taken together these changes suggest a family situation in which many high school seniors might be expected to show gains in educational achievement.

However, there were negative family elements as well. The average number of study aids, such as reference books, a daily newspaper, and a typewriter, available in high school seniors' homes declined during this decade. In particular, there was a decline in the availability of a place for students to study in their own homes. By 1982, only slightly more than half of high school seniors indicated they had a specific place at home to study.

We find, then, that during this decade many students met increasing educational expectations from their parents but did not find a comparable increase in other forms of home support for learning.

In looking at the students' aspirations, attitudes and values, we find increased educational aspirations among young women in 1982, as compared to 1972. We also see a widening gap in the educational aspirations of young people from different socioeconomic levels. This accounts for the otherwise somewhat paradoxical finding of more young people in 1982 planning to enter the labor force immediately after high school. By 1982, high school seniors were more self-confident than they had been a decade earlier. However, they were also less certain of their ability to control their futures. The 1982 seniors were more concerned with financial success than their 1972 counterparts; they also were less altruistic.

The 1972 and 1982 high school seniors had high educational and occupational aspirations, appeared self-confident, and were seeking futures in which they would be economically successful. If their school behaviors reflect these attitudes and values, we might expect to find conscientious students working diligently at achieving the academic success necessary for their life goals. We will see in Chapter 4 whether this behavior actually occurred.

Notes and References

1. COOPERATIVE INSTITUTIONAL RESEARCH PROGRAM (1986) *1986 Freshman Survey Results*, Los Angeles: University of California/American Council on Education.
2. LASCH, C. (1979) *The Culture of Narcissism: American Life in an Age of Diminishing Expectations.* New York: Norton.
3. YANKELOVICH, D. (1981) *New Rules: Searching for Self-Fulfillment in a World Turned Upside Down.* New York: Random House.

3   How Did the American High School Change Between 1972 and 1982?

The American high school was not immune to the political, social and economic changes discussed in the last chapter. Two movements, in particular, left their mark on the schools in the 1970s: one for greater equality in education and one for a more 'relevant' education program for an increasingly diverse student population.

The Supreme Court decision, *Brown v. Board of Education*, marked the beginning of a renewed national concern for social equality. Passage of the Civil Rights Act of 1964, the Elementary and Secondary Education Act of 1965, Title IX of the Education Amendments of 1972 and the Education for All Handicapped Children Act of 1975 increased the educational opportunities available to racial/ethnic minorities, to children with handicapping conditions, to women and to educationally disadvantaged students. High schools improved and broadened their offerings in special education, developed remedial education programs, provided new courses for non-English-speaking students, and broadened the participation of women in traditionally male courses and extracurricular activities, particularly in the areas of vocational education and sports.

As the student population became more diversified, and as students became more politicized in the late 1960s, education reformers called for alternative schools, electives and experience-based curricula to meet the needs and demands of *all* high school students. In an attempt to keep students in school and to retrieve dropouts, educators designed programs that were intended to be practical, interesting and relevant. To provide greater access to higher education, many colleges and universities lowered entrance standards. School districts, in turn, reduced their high school graduation course work requirements.

In this chapter, we look at changes in the typical high school in the United States between 1972 and 1982. Using data from the NLS-

72 and HS&B school and student questionnaires, we examine four aspects of the high school: (i) student body characteristics; (ii) characteristics of the teaching staff; (iii) educational programs and teaching methods; and (iv) students' ratings of the quality of their schools.

Student Body Characteristics

In both 1972 and 1982 the vast majority of US students attended public high schools. The proportion of seniors enrolled in public high schools and in Catholic high schools declined slightly, however, between 1972 and 1982, from 91 per cent to 89 per cent for the public sector and from 8 to 7 per cent for Catholic sector. At the same time, the proportion of students enrolled in private, non-Catholic high schools showed a corresponding increase.

There were major changes between 1972 and 1982 in the racial/ethnic composition of high schools, in the dropout rate, and in the proportion of graduates continuing on to college.

As shown in Table 11, in 1972, a majority (53 per cent) of high schools in the United States reported that all or nearly all of their students (95 per cent or more) were White. Eleven per cent of the high schools were 'majority-minority'; that is, less than 50 per cent of their student body was White. Most of the predominantly White high schools tended to be located in suburban or rural areas and served middle and upper socioeconomic status students. In contrast, the 'majority-minority' high schools primarily served low socioeconomic status students and were typically located in urban areas and in the South.

The schools that 1982 seniors attended as sophomores generally had the same racial composition as those attended by the 1972 seniors. Catholic schools provide the exception to this statement. The percentage of Catholic schools that were 50 to 94 per cent White nearly doubled between 1972 and 1980, while the percentage that were predominately White dropped from 60 per cent to 36 per cent. There was also a tendency for more low socioeconomic schools, schools in the Northeast and West, and schools in urban communities to fall into the 'majority-minority' category in 1980 than in 1972.

A recently published study by Orfield and his colleagues provides insight into the racial/ethnic characteristics of students who attend 'majority-minority' schools.[1] They report that in 1984, 64 per cent of Black students and 71 per cent of Hispanic students nationwide were enrolled in schools that were less than 50 per cent White. Nearly

Table 11   Percentage of high schools with various proportions of White students

	With 0–49%		With 50–79%		With 80–94%		With 95–100%	
	1972	1980*	1972	1980*	1972	1980*	1972	1980*
Total	10.9	11.5	14.5	15.2	21.8	19.8	52.8	53.5
School Type								
Public	11.4	12.6	15.6	15.9	20.5	18.4	52.5	53.1
Private	0.0	8.7	2.4	6.3	46.8	20.4	50.7	64.6
Catholic	6.6	6.7	10.8	24.8	22.7	32.9	59.9	35.7
Average SES of Students								
Low	22.7	38.0	24.4	11.5	22.0	13.7	30.9	36.9
Middle	6.8	3.6	11.1	20.0	17.2	16.3	64.8	60.1
High	1.5	1.2	6.6	9.2	33.8	33.1	58.1	56.5
Community Type								
Urban	24.4	26.9	20.2	20.2	25.0	21.9	30.4	30.9
Suburban	7.5	6.2	13.3	16.6	27.1	27.9	52.1	49.3
Rural	9.7	9.8	13.9	12.2	16.0	12.9	60.4	65.1
Region								
Northeast	4.4	5.8	6.0	10.9	18.9	24.2	70.6	59.1
Northcentral	5.8	3.3	3.1	4.1	15.6	12.1	75.5	80.5
South	20.4	20.1	21.6	27.1	29.6	20.4	28.4	32.4
West	8.4	14.2	32.8	15.2	20.5	26.5	38.2	44.1

* Represents percentage of White students in schools when students were sophomores.

one-third of the Blacks and Hispanics attended schools that were 'intensely segregated', that is, 90 per cent or more minority. The researchers found that the level of segregation of Black students was unchanged between 1972 and 1984, but that the percentage of Hispanic students attending 'majority-minority' schools climbed from 57 per cent in 1972 to 71 per cent in 1984. Given the high level of segregation, the authors warned against the 'deepening isolation of children growing up in inner-city ghettos and barrios from any contact with mainstream American society'.[2]

High school attrition was not a serious problem in many high schools in 1972. Nearly two-thirds of all high schools reported that fewer than four per cent of their tenth grade students dropped out of school before graduating from twelfth grade. The schools with the lowest dropout rates tended to be Catholic or other private high schools, schools serving middle and upper socioeconomic status students, and schools in the northeastern region of the country. Only about four per cent of all high schools reported a dropout rate greater than 20 per cent. Schools with high dropout rates tended to be public high schools, schools serving low SES students, schools in the South, and schools in urban areas.

By 1982, the dropout problem had become more serious in many high schools (See Table 12). Fewer than half of all high schools now

Table 12   Percentage of high schools with various proportions of dropouts (Students who entered grade 10 but did not complete grade 12)

	With 0–4%		With 5–9%		With 10–19%		With 20% or More	
	1972	1982	1972	1982	1972	1982	1972	1982
Total	62.2	48.5	20.8	24.9	13.4	19.1	3.6	7.5
School Type								
Pubic	58.2	41.5	23.3	30.3	15.0	21.8	3.6	6.5
Private	96.1	63.5	2.4	6.6	1.5	13.5	0.0	16.4
Catholic	97.1	93.1	0.5	4.2	1.8	2.0	0.0	0.7
Average SES of Students								
Low	38.8	35.5	32.0	26.3	22.9	25.4	6.3	12.8
Middle	71.9	44.3	15.1	31.0	9.8	19.1	3.1	5.6
High	78.3	68.5	15.9	10.8	5.6	14.0	0.1	6.8
Community Type								
Urban	61.0	49.3	13.9	13.4	13.5	22.8	11.6	14.6
Suburban	62.8	51.8	23.0	26.5	12.2	14.7	1.9	7.0
Rural	61.8	45.9	21.2	27.6	14.4	21.0	2.6	5.5
Region								
Northeast	73.0	60.1	19.8	26.2	5.1	10.4	10.4	3.3
Northcentral	78.8	50.1	10.8	21.1	8.1	26.2	2.3	2.5
South	46.6	43.5	21.4	28.8	26.4	19.3	5.5	8.4
West	49.6	44.2	40.9	23.2	5.7	14.9	3.8	17.7

had a dropout rate of 4 per cent or less. The percentage of schools with dropout rates over 20 per cent rose from 3.6 per cent in 1972 to 7.5 per cent in 1982. Dropout, which had traditionally been a problem for low SES schools and for urban high schools, had become a problem for high SES high schools and suburban high schools as well.

At the same time that fewer students were completing high school, high schools reported sending an increasing number of their graduates to two-year or four-year colleges. Between 1972 and 1982, the percentage of schools with 70 per cent or more of their graduates attending college increased from 9 per cent to 20 per cent. (See Table 13). The most dramatic increase occurred in Catholic high schools and in high SES schools. By 1982, nearly 80 per cent of Catholic high schools reported sending more than 70 per cent of their graduates on to two-year or four-year colleges, up from 34 per cent ten years earlier. In contrast, the increase in the percentage of public high schools reporting comparably high proportions of their graduates enrolled in postsecondary education was two percentage points, from 6 per cent to 8 per cent. Over 60 per cent of high schools with a high average socioeconomic status student body indicated that 70 per cent or more of their graduates went on to college, double the percentage reported in 1972. High college attendance rates were found in only

Table 13   Percentage of high schools with various proportions of last year's graudates now enrolled in a two-year or four-year college

	With 0–29%		With 30–49%		With 50–69%		With 70–100%	
	1972	1982	1972	1982	1972	1982	1972	1982
Total	30.6	21.3	34.9	33.5	25.3	24.8	9.3	20.4
School Type								
Public	33.1	24.2	38.2	38.5	22.8	29.2	5.9	8.0
Private	0.0	15.8	15.5	18.6	55.2	6.0	29.3	59.6
Catholic	9.4	0.0	18.1	7.9	38.3	19.4	34.2	79.0
Average SES of Students								
Low	58.1	40.0	30.9	35.9	9.7	21.7	1.4	2.4
Middle	19.9	18.7	43.2	43.5	30.2	28.6	6.7	9.2
High	11.4	9.6	19.0	9.4	39.3	19.4	30.4	61.5
Community Type								
Urban	21.8	14.2	29.5	24.9	29.3	18.2	19.4	42.6
Suburban	17.7	20.3	36.9	31.8	31.7	23.0	13.6	24.9
Rural	45.1	24.2	34.8	37.4	18.0	28.2	2.1	10.2
Region								
Northeast	20.1	10.3	34.3	27.9	27.3	27.2	18.3	34.6
Northcentral	24.8	15.0	43.3	41.4	27.0	30.7	4.9	12.9
South	39.0	28.0	29.9	29.0	21.8	22.8	9.3	20.2
West	37.2	29.6	29.6	33.5	26.9	16.3	6.3	20.6

two per cent of high schools with populations that were predominantly low in socioeconomic status.

These data suggest a widening gap among secondary schools in the United States, especially among schools serving students from different socioeconomic levels. Some schools experienced an increase in students who would not complete their high school education. Other schools found they had a growing group of students whose goal was postsecondary education.

Characteristics of the Teaching Staff

A major set of school factors that affects the quality of students' educational experiences is the nature of the school's faculty. Relatively comparable data were available from the NLS and the HS&B school questionnaires in three areas: (i) student/staff ratios; (ii) percentage of staff with advanced degrees; and (iii) teacher turnover rate.

The schools that 1982 seniors attended as sophomores generally had lower student/staff ratios than the schools that high school seniors in 1972 attended. Between 1972 and 1980, the average number of students per high school classroom teacher dropped from 17.6 to 14.7. (See Table 14.) This decline was significant for schools at all three

Table 14   *Number of students per teacher*

	1972	1980*
Total	17.6	14.7#
School Type		
Public	17.8	16.0#
Private	11.6	6.9
Catholic	17.9	17.8
Average SES of Students		
Low	17.6	15.0#
Middle	17.2	15.0#
High	18.9	15.0#
Community Type		
Urban	19.7	13.8#
Suburban	18.7	17.3#
Rural	15.9	13.2#
Region		
Northeast	16.9	15.2
Northcentral	16.1	14.9
South	17.7	14.8#
West	21.2	14.0#

* Represents student-teacher ratio in schools when students were sophomores.
\# Statistically significant decrease.

socioeconomic levels, in urban, suburban and rural communities, in public schools and in the South and West. The largest declines were typically found in schools with high socioeconomic student bodies, urban schools and schools in the South and West. By 1980, student/ staff ratios were comparable across schools grouped by socioeconomic status and region. Private non-Catholic schools had considerably smaller ratios than either public or Catholic schools and student/staff ratios tended to be larger in suburban than in either urban or rural schools.

One traditional measure of teacher quality is the level of formal education that teachers in a school have obtained. Nationally, the percentage of schools where the majority of the staff hold advanced degrees increased from 22 per cent to nearly 32 per cent between 1972 and 1980. (See Table 15.) The largest changes occurred in low socioeconomic schools, rural schools and schools located in the South. In each of these groups of schools, the percentage of schools where more than half of the staff held master's or doctor's degrees more than doubled, from 10 per cent to more than 20 per cent. In spite of these substantial gains, large disparities in the level of staff training remained in 1980. High socioeconomic schools, urban and suburban schools and schools in the Northeast were twice as likely to report that a majority of their teachers had advanced degrees than were schools with low socioeconomic student bodies, rural schools and

Table 15   Percentage of high schools with various proportions of teachers holding master's or doctor's degrees

	With 0–29%		With 30–49%		With 50–69%		With 70–100%	
	1972	1980*	1972	1980*	1972	1980*	1972	1980*
Total	47.9	36.3	30.0	32.1	15.2	19.9	6.9	11.7
School Type								
Public	51.2	36.6	28.5	31.2	14.2	18.8	6.2	13.4
Private	30.5	39.2	54.1	32.8	13.6	24.2	1.8	3.8
Catholic	18.8	27.6	37.8	39.1	28.1	22.3	15.3	11.0
Average SES of Students								
Low	69.8	36.1	20.0	39.9	7.2	11.3	3.0	12.7
Middle	43.4	41.4	34.0	29.2	15.6	19.0	6.9	10.4
High	22.6	21.2	36.7	30.6	27.4	32.7	13.3	15.5
Community Type								
Urban	31.9	33.5	37.7	23.3	20.7	26.6	9.8	16.5
Suburban	34.6	30.3	34.9	30.5	19.8	23.7	10.8	15.5
Rural	65.4	41.6	23.5	36.3	8.8	14.7	2.3	7.3
Region								
Northeast	29.5	20.3	30.9	21.8	23.5	26.0	16.1	31.9
Northcentral	49.2	40.7	30.1	31.6	14.5	16.0	6.3	11.7
South	55.5	38.6	32.2	34.0	10.9	21.3	1.4	6.1
West	52.5	39.2	24.5	38.2	15.3	18.2	8.0	4.3

* Percentage of teachers in schools with advanced degrees when students were sophomores.

schools in the southern, western or northcentral sections of the country.

Schools were also asked to report on the level of teacher turnover in their schools, specifically the percentage of full-time high school teachers who left their school for reasons other than death or retirement. In 1980, one-fifth of the high schools reported a turnover of more than 20 per cent of their teachers, a small increase from 1972. (See Table 16.) The problem of growing teacher turnover rates is magnified when one looks at the change in the percentage of schools with turnover rates of 10 per cent or more. Nationally, the figures increased from 38 per cent to 46 per cent. In urban communities, the percentages grew from 27 per cent to 40 per cent. By 1980, teacher turnover rates did not differ by the socioeconomic status of the school, but non-public schools, rural schools and schools in the Northcentral region of the country had a disproportionate number of schools with high staff turnover.

In summary, high schools in the early 1980s typically had smaller student/staff ratios and a better educated teaching staff than did high schools in the early 1970s. These benefits, however, were offset somewhat by a growing teacher turnover rate. While student/staff ratios

Table 16   Percentage of high schools with various proportions of teachers leaving since the end of the school year

	With 0–4%		With 5–9%		With 10–19%		With 20–100%	
	1972	*1980**	*1972*	*1980**	*1972*	*1980**	*1972*	*1980**
Total	46.8	38.1	15.4	15.7	20.3	26.1	17.5	20.1
School Type								
Public	47.7	41.4	16.3	16.1	19.0	25.4	17.0	17.0
Private	22.9	27.0	5.5	15.6	62.3	26.4	9.2	31.0
Catholic	52.2	25.8	9.8	12.2	8.8	31.9	29.2	30.1
Average SES of Students								
Low	51.2	43.3	12.3	7.7	15.3	24.7	21.3	24.3
Middle	42.7	35.4	17.7	19.1	23.5	25.4	16.1	20.2
High	50.2	37.3	14.4	17.1	20.3	28.1	15.1	17.4
Community Type								
Urban	57.1	44.6	16.0	15.9	14.0	23.3	12.9	16.2
Suburban	47.4	42.1	17.3	20.2	21.4	24.3	13.9	13.5
Rural	43.0	33.0	13.6	12.4	21.3	28.3	22.1	26.2
Region								
Northeast	54.1	55.1	20.2	18.8	20.6	17.9	5.1	8.2
Northcentral	40.2	30.9	14.4	16.0	20.5	27.0	24.9	26.1
South	44.3	33.9	14.7	13.5	21.7	32.3	19.3	20.3
West	56.0	42.4	12.6	16.4	16.5	20.5	14.9	20.7

* Teacher turnover rate in schools at the time the students were sophomores.

become comparable across most groups of schools by 1980, differences remained in the percentage of staff with advanced degrees and teacher turnover. Students attending low socioeconomic schools, rural schools and schools outside the Northeast were less likely to encounter well-educated and stable teaching forces.

Educational Programs and Teaching Methods

During the 1960s, high schools responded to an increasingly heterogeneous and politicized student body by diversifying their curriculum. The number of courses offered in American high schools doubled between 1960 and 1972. While advanced courses held their own or expanded somewhat during this period, most of the growth in curriculum was in remedial courses, courses in everyday living, and inter-disciplinary programs.[3] These changes continued into the 1970s. In this section, we look at changes in high school participation in selected programs — federal compensatory, bilingual and vocational education programs and advanced placement courses — and in the kinds of instructional methods used in high school classrooms.

The per cent of high schools participating in Title I of the

Table 17 *Percentage of high schools participating in selected federal programs*

	Title I		Title I-B		Title VII		Title I-F	
	1972	1982	1972	1982	1972	1982	1972	1982
Total	67.1	59.3#	62.5	57.3	6.9	15.1*	50.2	60.1*
School Type								
Public	75.1	72.5	70.4	71.4	8.0	19.4*	57.6	76.8*
Private	0.0	3.9	1.5	5.8	0.0	0.0	1.5	0.0
Catholic	14.8	22.8	7.3	9.2	0.5	0.2	0.8	2.5
Average SES of Students								
Low	89.0	71.6#	74.4	79.1	7.4	13.7	54.5	84.8*
Middle	61.8	70.2	60.2	61.1	7.7	16.6*	49.8	65.9*
High	41.5	24.4#	49.2	27.9#	3.8	13.4*	44.8	25.3#
Community Type								
Urban	33.2	29.0	54.2	44.7	8.2	22.6*	37.7	40.7
Suburban	62.1	51.6#	61.5	60.5	7.7	19.0*	49.5	57.2
Rural	82.9	74.4	66.0	59.1	5.6	10.1	55.3	68.7
Region								
Northeast	65.6	72.5	55.6	56.4	7.6	18.1*	38.3	43.1
Northcentral	66.9	70.5	55.8	54.5	4.6	10.1	45.9	64.1*
South	71.1	52.6#	66.7	64.1	6.1	14.9*	56.5	70.9*
West	60.8	40.3#	74.5	50.5#	11.4	21.3	59.5	48.2

* Statistically significant increase
# Statistically significant decrease

Elementary and Secondary Education Act (education of economically disadvantaged children) declined from 67 to 59 per cent between 1972 and 1982. The decline in participation was concentrated in low SES and high SES high schools while middle SES high schools showed a slight increase in participation (See Table 17). As a result, by 1982, participation rates were comparable for low and middle SES schools. The relatively low rate of participation by urban high schools in both 1972 and 1982 is related to federal provisions that target Title I funds to the poorest schools in districts with more than one high school, and to the tendency of large school districts to place most of their funds in elementary, rather than secondary, schools. Cuts in Title I funds in the early 1980s also led many districts (particularly those with extensive need) to end their high school Title I programs and to concentrate their resources in elementary schools.[4] These actions may account for the relatively large decline in Title I programs in high schools with low socioeconomic status student bodies.

At the same time, more high schools became involved in Title-VII of the Elementary and Secondary Education Act (bilingual education). Increased participation in bilingual education programs occurred primarily in public high schools and in urban and suburban high schools. Few non-public schools participated in this program.

The period 1972 to 1982 saw a decline in the percentage of high

Table 18   Percentage of high schools with selected courses and methods

	Advanced Placement		Ability Grouping	
	1972	*1982*	*1972*	*1982*
Total	15.0	35.7*	59.5	42.1#
School Type				
Public	14.3	33.7*	58.7	42.7#
Private	6.8	40.6	41.0	29.5
Catholic	25.4	47.7	72.8	55.8
Average SES of Students				
Low	5.8	16.6*	53.4	39.6#
Middle	13.7	30.7*	59.1	38.6#
High	31.7	64.8*	69.9	52.5#
Community Type				
Urban	32.0	55.9*	56.5	49.0
Suburban	19.5	47.2*	70.5	50.3#
Rural	3.9	21.2*	50.4	34.1#
Region				
Northeast	28.4	·61.7*	80.7	73.8
Northcentral	10.0	22.9*	46.6	26.8#
South	11.2	33.4*	58.3	44.2#
West	16.0	38.0*	58.5	33.8#

* Statistically significant increase
# Statistically significant decrease

schools participating in the vocational education basic program (Title I-B), but an increase in participation in the consumer and home-making education program (Title I-F). Increased participation in Title I-F occurred primarily in public high schools and in schools serving low and middle socioeconomic status students. Decreased involvement in the basic vocational education program was concentrated in high SES schools.

The schools also changed in the types of courses offered and in the teaching methods employed. Data about the availability of advanced placement courses and about the use of ability grouping methods are provided in Table 18 as examples of these changes.

There was a dramatic increase in the percentage of high schools offering advanced placement courses, a program that provides able students with the opportunity to earn college credit. This change was significant across region, community type and socioeconomic status of the student body. At both points in time, however, advanced placement courses were more likely to be available in Catholic high schools, schools with high SES students, schools in urban and suburban areas, and schools in the northeast than in other high schools.

Ability grouping, used to divide students into classroom groups of similar achievement levels, declined in use during the 1972 and 1982

Table 19 Student reported use of instructional methods
(Scale: from 1 = Never to 4 = Frequently)

Instructional Method	Mean Response 1972	1980*
Listening to Teachers' Lectures	3.26	3.27
Writing Essays, Themes, etc.	2.85	2.82
Student-centered Discussions	2.73	2.67#
Work on Project or in Lab	2.48	2.37#
Individualized Instruction	1.98	2.09**
Teaching Machines or CAI	1.48	1.62**

* Frequency of these instructional methods when the students were sophomores.
\# Statistically significant decrease.
** Statistically significant increase.

decade. At both points in time, ability grouping was most likely to be found in Catholic high schools, in high schools serving high SES students, and in high schools located in the northeast.

These data suggest a widening gap in the kind of educational programs available in different types of high schools. Schools serving middle class students were offering more programs for disadvantaged students, while these programs were declining in schools serving the less affluent as well as the more affluent. Schools serving high SES students were providing less vocational education, while these programs increased in schools for middle and low SES students. The availability of advanced placement courses increased markedly in schools serving the most affluent students and in non-public schools. The use of ability grouping declined but, as we shall see later, similar effects may have been obtained by curriculum tracking.

In addition to collecting information on selected school programs, the two surveys asked students how often they experienced six different instructional methods in their schools: listening to teachers' lectures; participating in student-centered discussions; working on a project or in a laboratory; writing essays, themes, poetry or stories; having individualized instruction; and using teaching machines or computer-assisted instruction.

Table 19 summarizes the mean responses for students in 1972 and in 1980. The most frequently used instructional method in both years was listening to lectures by the teacher. Students reported that they wrote essays, themes, etc. and engaged in student-centered discussions fairly often, but rarely used individualized instruction, teaching machines or computer-assisted instruction. There were small, but statistically significant, decreases in the use of student-centered discussions and work on projects or in laboratories between 1972 and 1980,

Table 20 Students' ratings of their high schools: Areas showing improvement
(*Scale*: from 1 = poor to 4 = excellent)

	Teacher Interest		Library		Academic Instruction	
	1972	1982	1972	1982	1972	1982
Total	2.52	2.72*	2.74	2.86*	2.78	2.84*
School Type						
Public	2.49	2.67*	2.75	2.87*	2.76	2.80*
Private	2.95	3.30	2.85	2.89	2.95	3.27
Catholic	2.82	3.12*	2.55	2.65	3.01	3.15*
SES						
Low	2.52	2.62*	2.79	2.84	2.69	2.71
Middle	2.51	2.70*	2.73	2.86*	2.78	2.83
High	2.55	2.87*	2.71	2.87*	2.84	3.00*
Community Type						
Urban	2.54	2.71*	2.79	2.89*	2.80	2.83
Suburban	2.52	2.76*	2.74	2.88*	2.80	2.90*
Rural	2.52	2.67*	2.68	2.80*	2.70	2.75
Region						
Northeast	2.53	2.73*	2.73	2.87*	2.85	2.89
Northcentral	2.49	2.69*	2.72	2.87*	2.75	2.83*
South	2.54	2.71*	2.76	2.85*	2.75	2.81
West	2.55	2.80*	2.75	2.83*	2.75	2.86*

* Statistically significant increase

and small, but statistically significant, increases in the use of individualized instruction, teaching machines and computer-assisted instruction.

Some variations appear when students are grouped by demographic characteristics. For example, the use of lectures and the frequency of writing essays, themes, etc. increased somewhat in academic programs, among high socioeconomic students and in Catholic schools between 1972 and 1980. Low socioeconomic students, Black students and students in the vocational education curriculum reported writing less and participating less often in student-centered discussions in 1980 than in 1972.

Students' Ratings of Their Schools

A final look at the differences in high schools in 1972 and 1982 comes from the seniors' ratings of their schools. Did these students feel they were receiving high quality instruction, that their teachers were interested in them, that the reputation of their school was high, and that the library and physical plant were adequate?

The results, shown in Tables 20 and 21, present a mixed picture.

Table 21   Students' ratings of their high schools: Areas showing declines
(*Scale:* from 1 = poor to 4 = excellent)

	Reputation in Community		Condition of Building	
	1972	1982	1972	1982
Total	2.99	2.90#	2.86	2.82#
School Type				
Public	2.96	2.84#	2.85	2.80#
Private	3.34	3.38	3.04	3.18
Catholic	3.37	3.43	3.02	2.95
SES				
Low	2.86	2.73#	2.74	2.69
Middle	2.99	2.88#	2.86	2.81
High	3.12	3.11	2.98	2.97
Community Type				
Urban	2.90	2.78#	2.79	2.74
Suburban	3.06	2.97#	2.93	2.88#
Rural	2.95	2.87#	2.79	2.79
Region				
Northeast	3.04	2.87#	2.91	2.84#
Northcentral	2.93	2.94	2.85	2.87#
South	3.06	2.89#	2.83	2.78#
West	2.91	2.91	2.84	2.79#

Statistically significant decrease

The overall level of all the ratings is on the positive side of the scale's 2.5 midpoint, showing that the students feel their schools are 'good'. The mean rating increased slightly, from 2.78 in 1972 to 2.83, indicating a modest improvement in the students' perception of their schools. However, there were declines in two aspects of the school, reputation in the community and condition of the building. These declines were balanced by increases in ratings of teacher interest in students, adequacy of the library, and quality of academic instruction. All of the changes in ratings for the total group of students, both positive and negative, were statistically significant.

The largest increase in students' ratings of their high schools occurred in the amount of interest teachers showed in the students. At both points in time, seniors in non-public schools felt their teachers were more interested in them than did seniors in public high schools. While students of all socioeconomic levels reported an increase in teacher interest, this increase was largest for high SES students. The next largest increase occurred on students' ratings of the quality of their school library. High and middle SES students reported more improvement than did low SES students. The third area of improvement, according to the student ratings, was in the quality of academic instruction. However, this increase was significant only for high SES students, not for middle and low income students.

Two of the areas rated by the students showed declines. These were the schools' reputation in the community and the condition of the school building. Declines in the reputation of the school were found only for public high schools; students in non-public schools rated their schools was having a better reputation in 1982 than in 1972. Significant declines in the reputation of their high school were found for low and middle SES students only; there was essentially no change in high income students' reputational ratings of their high schools. Declines in ratings of the condition of high school buildings were statistically significant only in public high schools, schools in the northeast, and in suburban high schools.

These student ratings, like the data on student body characteristics and on school programs, indicate the growing differences between schools in the United States. Students in non-public schools indicate much higher levels of teacher interest in students, better academic instruction, and a better school reputation in their communities than do public school students. Students from the most affluent families report much greater increases in teacher interest and in the quality of academic instruction than students from middle and low SES families. In addition, students from these high SES families report no decline in their schools' reputations in the communities, while middle and low SES students report significant decreases.

Summary

The evidence in this chapter suggests that high schools changed during the decade of the 1970s, but in somewhat inconsistent ways. At the same time that high schools sent more of their students on to college, dropout rates increased. While high schools reported smaller teacher/student ratios, better educated teaching staffs and a greater participation in the advanced placement program, teacher turnover rates were on the rise.

The data also suggest that high schools became increasingly different between 1972 and 1982. For example, by 1982, low SES schools were two to three times more likely to have a 'majority-minority' student body and high dropout rates, and half as likely to have a majority of their graduates attending college as the typical high school. Low SES schools had above average participation rates in federal compensatory education programs, but below average participation rates in the advanced placement program. The contrast between low and high SES schools was even more stark.

Notes and References

1. ORFIELD, G. (1987) 'School Segregation in the 1980'. Chicago, University of Chicago National School Desegregation Project.
2. *Ibid.*
3. POWELL A. G., FARRAR, E. and COHEN, D. K. (1985) *The Shopping Mall High School*, Boston, Houghton Mifflin Company.
4. GOERTZ, M. (1987) *School Districts' Allocation of Chapter 1 Resources.* Final report to the US Department of Education, Contract No. 400-85-1030. Princeton, NJ, Educational Testing Service.

4   Changes in Students' School
        Experiences

In the preceding two chapters we saw how high school seniors and the schools themselves changed from 1972 to 1982. In this chapter we will explore what these self-confident and success-oriented young people did in high school. Was their behavior consistent with their aspriations and attitudes? We search for answers to this question by looking at curriculum track, course-taking behavior, the amount of time students spent doing homework, and their participation in extracurricular activities.

Curriculum

Curriculum is one of the first, and most important, decisions made when a student enters high school. Curriculum requirements and practices often determine many of the courses that students take. Curriculum and ability grouping are two of the most common forms of tracking in high schools. As Oakes has pointed out, 'on the basis of these sorting decisions, the groups of students that result, and the way that educators see the students in these groups, teenagers are treated by and experience schools very differently'.[1]

About 46 per cent of 1972 high school seniors were enrolled in an academic, or college-preparatory, curriculum; 32 per cent were in a general curriculum and 22 per cent were in a vocational curriculum. By 1982, the proportion of seniors in the academic curriculum had declined while the proportion in the general and vocational curricula had increased; about 38 per cent of the 1982 seniors were in the academic curriculum track, 35 per cent in the general curriculum, and 27 per cent in a vocational curriculum (See Table 22).

Table 22   Percentage of high school seniors in each curriculum track

	1972			1982		
	Acad.	Gen.	Voc.	Acad.	Gen.	Voc.
Total	45.7	31.8	22.4	38.3	35.1	26.6
Sex						
Male	48.3	33.1	18.6	36.7	37.8	25.5
Female	43.2	30.6	26.3	39.9	32.3	27.8
SES						
Low	25.2	39.6	35.2	21.2	40.5	38.4
Middle	45.0	32.1	22.8	35.1	36.8	28.1
High	68.1	23.3	8.6	61.8	26.3	12.0
Race/Ethnicity						
White	48.6	30.6	20.8	40.5	34.8	24.7
Black	32.7	34.2	33.1	32.4	32.9	34.7
Mexican American	23.7	44.8	31.5	22.5	42.5	34.9
Puerto Rican	37.3	33.9	28.8	29.3	40.2	30.5
Other Hispanic	36.9	37.7	25.4	28.6	38.9	32.5
Asian American	53.5	33.7	12.8	55.1	26.1	18.8
American Indian	23.5	39.4	37.0	15.8	53.2	31.0
School Type						
Public	43.8	33.7	22.5	34.6	36.9	28.6
Private	75.1	20.2	4.6	70.3	19.5	10.2
Catholic	70.8	14.9	14.3	71.4	19.3	9.4

The shift out of the academic curriculum was greater among males, middle SES students, Whites, Hispanic students other than Mexican Americans, and public school students. Asian American students and students in Catholic schools were more likely to be in the academic curriculum in 1982 than in 1972.

The variations in curriculum by socioeconomic status and by race-ethnicity confirm what Oakes has reported. 'Poor and minority students are most likely to be placed at the lowest levels of the schools' sorting system.'[2] For example, in 1972 more than two-thirds of high SES students were in the academic curriculum track but only about one quarter of low SES students were in this curriculum. By 1982 both high and low SES groups had fewer students in the academic curriculum but high SES students were four times as likely to be in this curriculum track as low SES students.

What is the process by which students arrive in these curricular tracks? Kirst reports that in California 'students are generally assigned to the tracks based on criteria such as past performance, test scores, and teacher recommendations. ... The initial placement in a track and the suggestions for courses are mainly the responsibility of the school counselors'[3] Similar curricular track placement criteria are described by Oakes[4]. 'Almost universally, three kinds of information are taken into consideration, although in varying degrees in different schools.

These three are scores on standardized tests, teacher and counselor recommendations (including grades), and students' and their parents' choices'.

The 1982 students could indicate on the HS&B questionnaire if they had been assigned to a curriculum track, had chosen the curriculum alone, or had chosen the curriculum with the assistance of parent(s), teachers, guidance counselors, and/or friends. In an analysis of public high school guidance counseling, using the 1982 HS&B data, Ekstrom[5] found that 43 per cent of students in the general curriculum had been assigned to this track, as contrasted with 37 per cent of students in the vocational curriculum and 33 per cent of students in the academic curriculum. Minority students were more likely to be assigned to a curriculum track while White students were more likely to choose their curriculum. For example, 52 per cent of Black public high school students indicated that they had been assigned to a curriculum, while 58 per cent of White public high school students chose their curriculum track. Thus we find that track is prescribed for some students, especially minority students, while majority students are more likely to be offered a choice of curriculum.

Minority students are less likely to receive guidance counselor assistance in making a curriculum track choice than are White students. The analysis of the 1982 HS&B data shows that about 23 per cent of White public high school students receive guidance counselor assistance in making a curricular track choice, while only 20 per cent of Black students and 16 per cent of Mexican American students receive counselor help in making this choice. Students who do not receive counselor assistance are more likely be in nonacademic curricula. This is, in part, because many students are unaware of the consequences of their academic choices. Students who may need guidance most, since they come from homes where knowledge of the consequences of curriculum choices is limited, are least likely to receive such guidance in their high schools.[6]

Unfortunately, counselors are not always objective when making curriculum assignments or recommendations. Research indicates that counselors appear to be influenced by student language, dress and behavior when they assign students to a curriculum.[7] 'My hunch', says Oakes, 'is that, given the circumstances of placement decisions, factors often influenced by race and class — dress, speech patterns, ways of interacting with adults, and other behaviors — often do affect subjective judgments of academic aptitude and probably academic futures, and that educators allow this to happen quite unconsciously.'[8]

Curricular track is not always congruent with students' plans and expectations. Ekstrom[9] found that only 46 per cent of public high school students who expected, when they were in grade 9, that they would attend college were actually enrolled in a college-preparatory curriculum in grade 10. About half of all White students who planned to attend college were in the academic curricular track but only 34 per cent of Black students and 29 per cent of Mexican American students with college expectations were in an academic curriculum.

Regardless of how a student arrives at a curricular track and how well it matches her/his plans, this curricular decision will play a major role in determining what courses the student takes during high school.

Course-Taking

The National Commission on Excellence in Education[10] recommended, in 1983, that all high school students 'be required to lay the foundations in the Five New Basics by taking the following curriculum during their four years of high school: (i) 4 years of English; (ii) 3 years of mathematics; (iii) 3 years of science; (iv) 3 years of social studies; and (v) one-half year of computer science.' In this section we look at the actual level of course-taking among high school seniors in 1972 and 1982 and make some comparisons to this recommendation.

The average 1982 high school senior took fewer semesters of the 'New Basics', English, social studies, mathematics, science, and foreign languages, in grades 10–12 than the typical senior in 1972. However, there was an increase in the number of semesters of vocational education instruction (business, home economics, trade and industrial arts, etc.). These changes, which are based on an analysis of student transcripts in 1982 and on reports from the high schools in 1972, are summarized in Table 23 and shown in detail in Tables 24 through 29. Subjects in which the amount of instruction is frequently mandated by the state (e.g., English, social studies) showed less decline than subjects which are not under such control. The magnitude of the changes in course-taking across the decade can best be illustrated by pointing out that in 1972 the typical high school senior took more semesters of English than of any other subject. By 1982, however, the typical student took more semesters of vocational education than of English, social studies, mathematics, or science.

The largest negative change in course-taking behavior involved foreign languages. The decline of 1.2 semesters, or nearly half of the amount of foreign language instruction received in 1972, was consis-

Table 23 Mean number of semesters of instruction taken by high school seniors in selected subjects in grades 10–12

Subject	1972	1982	Difference
English	5.83	5.64	−.19*
Social Studies	5.21	4.96	−.26*
Mathematics	3.93	3.70	−.23*
Science	3.71	2.98	−.38*
Vocational Education	3.35	5.79	2.24*
Foreign Languages	2.64	1.45	−1.18*

* Difference significant at or beyond .05 level

Table 24 Mean number of semesters of English taken in grades 10–12

	1972	1982	Difference
Sex			
Males	5.82	5.62	−0.20*
Females	5.84	5.66	−0.18*
SES			
Low	5.80	5.67	−0.13*
Middle	5.81	5.62	−0.19*
High	5.91	5.70	−0.21*
Race/Ethnicity			
White	5.84	5.60	−0.24*
Black	5.82	5.89	0.07
Mexican American	5.64	5.57	−0.07
Puerto Rican	6.01	5.95	−0.06
Other Hispanic	5.74	5.77	0.03
Asian American	5.87	5.65	−0.22
American Indian	5.56	5.82	0.25
School Type			
Public	5.82	5.62	−0.20*
Private	6.48	5.81	−0.67*
Catholic	5.89	5.87	−0.02
Curriculum			
Academic	5.93	5.80	−0.13*
General	5.81	5.61	−0.20*
Vocational	5.65	5.49	−0.16*

* Difference significant at or beyond .05 level

tent as well as statistically significant across almost all population subgroups (Table 28).

The second largest decrease was in the number of science courses taken. This decline affected all subgroups except Asian American students (Table 27). The pattern of reduced instruction in science added to the existing gap in the educational experience of more and less affluent students (with the gap widening from 0.86 semesters less science in 1972 to 1.29 semesters less science in 1982). A growing difference in science education is also seen when comparing students

Table 25   Mean number of semesters of social studies taken in grades 10–12

	1972	1982	Difference
Sex			
Male	5.26	4.95	−0.31*
Female	5.17	4.96	−0.20*
SES			
Low	5.21	4.92	−0.29*
Middle	5.23	4.94	−0.28*
High	5.20	5.04	−0.16*
Race/Ethnicity			
White	5.21	4.98	−0.23*
Black	5.25	4.92	−0.33*
Mexican American	5.19	4.94	−0.26
Puerto Rican	5.57	4.76	−0.81*
Other Hispanic	4.92	4.98	0.06
Asian American	5.38	4.67	−0.72*
American Indian	5.04	4.79	−0.25
School Type			
Public	5.22	4.94	−0.28*
Private	4.92	4.93	0.01
Catholic	5.12	5.17	0.04
Curriculum			
Academic	5.26	5.03	−0.23*
General	5.29	5.06	−0.23*
Vocational	5.01	4.74	−0.27*

* Difference significant at or beyond .05 level

Table 26   Mean number of semesters of mathematics taken in grades 10–12

	1972	1982	Difference
Sex			
Male	4.22	3.88	−0.35*
Female	3.63	3.52	−0.11
SES			
Low	3.45	3.08	−0.37*
Middle	3.88	3.66	−0.22*
High	4.47	4.41	−0.06
Race/Ethnicity			
White	3.97	3.69	−0.28*
Black	3.86	3.85	−0.01
Mexican American	3.30	3.25	−0.05
Puerto Rican	4.09	4.01	−0.08
Other Hispanic	4.12	3.53	−0.59
Asian American	4.28	4.55	0.26
American Indian	2.67	3.25	0.58
School Type			
Public	3.86	3.59	−0.27*
Private	5.26	4.53	−0.72
Catholic	4.50	4.67	0.17
Curriculum			
Academic	4.72	4.77	0.05
General	3.34	3.22	−0.13
Vocational	2.97	2.78	−0.18

* Difference significant at or beyond .05 level

Table 27   Mean number of semesters of science taken in grades 10–12

	1972	1982	Difference
Sex			
Male	3.93	3.10	−0.84*
Female	3.48	2.86	−0.62*
SES			
Low	3.30	2.46	−0.85*
Middle	3.67	2.86	−0.81*
High	4.16	3.75	−0.41*
Race/Ethnicity			
White	3.77	3.04	−0.73*
Black	3.52	2.77	−0.75*
Mexican American	2.96	2.53	−0.42*
Puerto Rican	3.67	2.98	−0.69
Other Hispanic	3.80	2.60	−1.20*
Asian American	3.82	4.00	0.18
American Indian	2.75	2.42	−0.33
School Type			
Public	3.67	2.88	−0.79*
Private	4.71	3.72	−0.99*
Catholic	4.12	3.91	−0.21
Curriculum			
Academic	4.44	4.14	−0.30*
General	3.22	2.49	−0.73*
Vocational	2.75	1.93	−0.83*

* Difference significant at or beyond .05 level

Table 28   Mean number of semesters of vocational education taken in grades 10–12

	1972	1982	Difference
Sex			
Male	2.88	5.03	2.16*
Female	3.82	6.14	2.32*
SES			
Low	4.40	7.02	2.62*
Middle	3.49	5.85	2.36*
High	2.00	3.69	1.69*
Race/Ethnicity			
White	3.28	5.54	2.26*
Black	3.60	5.82	2.22*
Mexican American	3.44	6.12	2.68*
Puerto Rican	4.86	6.13	1.27
Other Hispanic	3.51	6.08	2.56*
Asian American	2.89	3.22	0.33
American Indian	4.51	5.78	1.27
School Type			
Public	3.43	5.86	2.43*
Private	0.52	2.24	1.72*
Catholic	2.34	3.60	1.26*
Curriculum			
Academic	1.78	3.29	1.50*
General	3.86	5.87	2.01*
Vocational	5.81	8.64	2.83*

* Difference significant at or beyond .05 level

Table 29   Mean number of semesters of foreign languages taken in grades 10–12

	1972	1982	Difference
Sex			
Male	2.38	1.20	−1.18*
Female	2.88	1.70	−1.18*
SES			
Low	1.79	0.78	−1.00*
Middle	2.56	1.35	−1.21*
High	3.47	2.33	−1.14*
Race/Ethnicity			
White	2.70	1.51	−1.20*
Black	2.07	1.02	−1.05*
Mexican American	2.23	1.38	−0.85*
Puerto Rican	3.24	1.55	−1.70*
Other Hispanic	3.87	1.45	−2.42*
Asian American	3.19	2.76	−0.44
American Indian	1.37	0.57	−0.80
School Type			
Public	2.50	1.30	−1.21*
Private	4.75	2.90	−1.86*
Catholic	3.88	2.77	−1.10*
Curriculum			
Academic	3.53	2.60	−0.94*
General	1.75	0.87	−0.88*
Vocational	1.35	0.54	−0.81*

* Difference significant at or beyond .05 level

in the academic and vocational curricula and between public and Catholic high school students. Academic students had 1.69 more semesters of science in 1972 and 2.21 more semesters in 1982. The difference between public and Catholic school students increased from 0.45 to 1.03 semesters.

There were comparable overall decreases in the amount of course work taken by students in social studies and in mathematics. In both of these subject areas we find that Catholic high school students showed slight increases in the amount of course-work taken while public high school students showed decreases. Males showed larger declines in course-taking in both subject areas than did females.

Mathematics is an area of special interest because of its importance as a prerequisite for entering many scientific and technical fields. Mathematics course-taking increased among some subgroups in the 1970s, specifically Asian American and American Indian students, students in Catholic high schools and students enrolled in an academic curriculum, while other subgroups and the total population showed declines in the amount of mathematics instruction they received. This resulted in a further widening of the gap in amount of mathematics instruction received by students in the different curricular tracks and by students in public and Catholic high schools. The gap between males and females in the number of mathematics courses narrowed, however.

Course-taking in English changed less than any other subject area, probably because most states mandate three or four years of English in grades 9–12. In contrast to the course-taking declines in other subjects, the decline in English is slightly larger for middle and high SES students than for low SES students. The decline is also somewhat greater for students in the general curriculum track than for students in academic and vocational curricula.

Direct comparisons between these data and the recommendations of the National Commission are difficult since the recommendations cover grades 9 to 12 and our data are for grades 10 to 12. Nevertheless, it appears that, both in 1972 and 1982, the typical high school student took fewer courses in most areas of the New Basics than the Commission has recommended. An exception may be social studies, where course-taking appears to be at or somewhat above the level recommended by the Commission.

In contrast to the declines in course-taking in the core academic subjects, we find a large rise in the number of semesters of instruction taken by students in vocational subjects. The increase in vocational education courses occurred among all groups of students. Not surprisingly the increase was greatest among students in the vocational curriculum track, but there were also significant increases for students in the academic and the general curricula. Mexican American students and low SES students also showed large increases in enrollment in vocational education courses. Public high school students showed greater increases in vocational course-taking than did students in non-public schools.

Information about the specific course areas within vocational education is available for public high school students. These data, showing the percentage of students in each curriculum track taking one or more courses in each vocational education category, are summarized in Table 30.

Most public high school students took one or more courses in vocational education. Business courses were the most popular; these were taken by about three-quarters of all public high school students. Home economics courses ranked second in popularity; these courses were especially popular with females, low SES students, and with Black and Hispanic students. For example, while only 35 per cent of White students in the academic curriculum took one or more courses in home economics, 53 per cent of Black students and 46 per cent of

Table 30   Percentage of 1982 public high school seniors taking one or more courses in
selected areas of vocational education

	Academic	General	Vocational
Total	90.0	96.1	98.1
Agriculture	5.4	13.1	13.5
Business, Office & Marketing	78.7	77.2	75.0
Construction	2.4	5.7	7.6
Home Economics	37.2	58.7	54.8
Industrial Arts	13.5	22.4	22.7
Mechanics & Repairs	6.8	15.0	16.2
Metal & Wood	13.9	24.2	22.2
Technology & Engineering	1.0	1.3	0.6

Mexican American students in this curriculum reported taking some home economics.

The exact reasons for differential course-taking by students are unknown. Curriculum track, of course, plays a large role, especially for academic students where course patterns tend to be more highly prescribed than in the general curriculum. Program planning guidance also plays a role. Lee and Ekstrom[11] found that approximately half of all public high school students received no guidance counselor assistance in planning their high school program. Minority and low SES high school students were significantly less likely to receive this type of guidance counselor assistance than majority and more affluent students.

While differences in course taking are, in part, related to curriculum track placement, there appear to be other influences at work as well. Course-taking in mathematics by general curriculum students is an example. Ekstrom[12] found that while only 39 per cent of White students in the general curriculum took general mathematics, 63 per cent of the Black students in this curriculum took this course; in contrast, 60 per cent of the White students in the general curriculum took Algebra I but only 44 per cent of the Black students.

These differences in course-taking determine, in large part, what and how much students learn in high school. As Oakes[13] has commented, 'Students can learn *in school* only those things that the school exposes them to'.

Curriculum and course-taking go hand-in-hand. Oakes found that the course content in low-track classes tended to be so limited that it essentially locked students into that track level. 'Many of the topics taught almost exclusively to students in low-track classes may be desirable learnings for all students — consumer math skills, for example. But these topics were taught to the exclusion of others —

Table 31   Percentage of high school seniors participating in selected extracurricular activities.

	1972	1982	Difference
Athletics	44.9	52.1	7.2*
Debate and/or Music	33.1	34.3	1.2
Subject Matter Clubs	25.6	20.4	−5.2*
Vocational Education Clubs	22.3	23.6	1.3*
Newspaper and/or Yearbook	20.2	18.6	−1.6*
Student Government	19.4	16.3	−3.1*
Hobby Clubs	18.7	20.0	1.3*
Cheerleading	17.3	13.7	−3.6*
Honorary Clubs	14.4	15.6	1.2*

* Difference significant at or beyond .05 level

introduction to algebraic equations, for example — that constitute prerequisite knowledge and skills for access to classes in different, and higher, level tracks. So, by the omission of certain content from low-track classes, students in effect were denied the opportunity to learn material essential for mobility among track levels'.[14]

In the next chapter we will see how the differences in curriculum and course-taking experience manifest themselves in educational outcome indicators such as tested achievement.

Extracurricular Activities

Students do not spend all their school time in the classroom. Extracurricular activities also play an important role in high schools. They not only serve as a social outlet but also provide a way for students to acquire skills and knowledge that may not be taught in the classroom.

Table 31 shows participation rates in selected extracurricular activities in 1972 and 1982. At both points in time athletics was by far the most popular extracurricular activity, involving approximately half of all high school seniors by 1982. Participation in athletics showed a marked increase in this decade, primarily because of increased participation by females and by Hispanic students. Cheerleading showed a decline in participation, most dramatically among young women.

Debating and musical activities (such as band and glee club) involved approximately one-third of all high school seniors. There was little change in participation in this activitiy across groups; increases were found primarily among females and vocational curriculum students.

Subject matter clubs showed the largest decline in student participation from 1972 to 1982. This decline is of particular concern since

Table 32   Time seniors spent each week doing homework
(*Scale*: 1 = 0 to 5 hours per week to 3 = more than 10 hours per week)

	1972	1982	Difference
Total	1.41	1.39	−0.01
Sex			
Male	1.30	1.31	0.01
Female	1.51	1.48	−0.03
SES			
Low	1.38	1.29	−0.09*
Middle	1.38	1.35	−0.04*
High	1.48	1.59	0.11*
Race/Ethnicity			
White	1.40	1.40	0.00
Black	1.45	1.38	−0.07*
Mexican American	1.32	1.29	−0.03
Puerto Rican	1.48	1.27	−0.21
Other Hispanic	1.46	1.36	−0.10
Asian American	1.71	1.82	0.11
American Indian	1.34	1.26	−0.08
School Type			
Public	1.39	1.36	−0.04*
Private	1.63	1.83	0.20
Catholic	1.54	1.66	0.12*
Curriculum			
Academic	1.55	1.66	0.11*
General	1.27	1.23	−0.05*
Vocational	1.31	1.24	−0.07*

these clubs offer students the opportunity to increase or enhance the knowledge they have acquired in the classroom. This decline occurred primarily among males and students in the general curriculum. Vocational education and hobby clubs, by contrast, showed small increases in participation rates across the decade.

There was also a decline in student participation in school newspaper and yearbooks and in student government. Participation in honorary clubs showed a slight increase.

Homework

The typical high school senior spent slightly less time doing homework in 1982 than did the typical 1972 senior. However, this decline is very small and is neither statistically nor practically significant. The means, shown in Table 32, were 1.41 in 1972 and 1.39 in 1982. These translate into slightly under five hours of homework per week, or approximately one hour per school day.

There were, however, some important subgroup differences in the amount of homework done. Middle and low SES students did significantly less homework in 1982 than 1972 while high SES students show a significant increase across the decade in the time they spent doing homework. These changes increased the existing difference in the amount of out-of-school time more and less affluent students devoted to study. In 1972, low SES students did about 24 minutes less homework per week than high SES students; by 1982 low SES students were doing about 30 minutes less homework per week than high SES students. The SES differences are paralleled in the high school curricular tracks. Academic curriculum students showed an increase in time spent on homework while, in contrast, general and vocational curriculum students reduced their homework time. Students in public high schools showed a small, but statistically significant, decrease in the amount of homework done while students in non-public schools reported doing an increased amount of homework.

Summary

In Chapter 2 we saw that both the 1972 and 1982 high school seniors had high educational aspirations and the desire for future success. This suggested that we would find many students in a college-preparatory curriculum, taking courses and participating in other school activities that would prepare them for college and their future careers.

Instead, we find that, despite aspirations for postsecondary education, less than half of the students are enrolled in an academic curriculum and the typical senior spends only about one hour per school day on homework.

Changes from 1972 to 1982 resulted in a substantial decrease in the proportion of high school seniors in the academic curriculum. These same changes also resulted in a large increase in the number of vocational education courses taken by high school seniors and a decrease in the number of courses taken in the 'New Basics'.

In the next chapter we will look at how these different educational experiences affected educational outcome indicators, specifically grades and tested achievement.

Notes and References

1. OAKES, J. (1985), *Keeping Track: How Schools Structure Inequality*, New Haven: Yale University Press, p. 3.
2. Ibid., p. 67.

3. KIRST, M. W. (1984) *California High School — Curriculum Study: Paths Through High School — Executive Summary*. Report prepared for the California Department of Education, January 5, 1984.
4. Oakes, *op. cit.*, p. 9.
5. EKSTROM, R. B. (1985) *Public High School Guidance Counseling: A Report to the College Board Commission on Precollege Guidance and Counseling*, Princeton: Educational Testing Service.
6. LEE, V. E. and EKSTROM, R. B. (1987) 'Student access to guidance counseling in high school', *American Educational Research Journal*, 24, 2, pp. 287–310.
7. CICOUREL, A. V. and KITSUSE, J. I. (1963) *The Educational Decision-makers*. Indianapolis: Bobbs-Merrill.
8. Oakes, *op. cit.*, p. 13.
9. Ekstrom, *op. cit.*
10. THE NATIONAL COMMISSION ON EXCELLENCE IN EDUCATION (1983) *A Nation at Risk: The Imperative for Educational Reform*, Washington, DC: US Department of Education.
11. Leep and Ekstrom, *op. cit.*
12. Ekstrom, *op. cit.*
13. Oakes, *op. cit.*, p. 73.
14. Oakes, *op. cit.*, p. 78.

5 Educational Outcomes or Why Did Test Scores Decline Between 1972 and 1982?

The previous three chapters have shown many changes in American high school seniors, their schools and their educational experiences in the decade between 1972 and 1982. In this chapter we investigate the extent to which these changes were reflected in educational outcome indicators, especially in achievement test scores.

Perhaps the most crucial question that can be asked about these high school seniors is 'How much did they learn from these schools and their educational experiences?' The best evidence of student learning comes from high school grades and from test scores.

Grades

The evidence about changes in curriculum and course-taking shows that, on average, the 1982 high school seniors were involved in less demanding curricular tracks and courses than their 1972 counterparts. One consequence of this, if grading standards are absolute, might be a decline in high school grades between 1972 and 1982. Alternatively, the easier course of study may lead to the 1982 students receiving higher grades.

On the NLS-72 and HS&B questionnaires, the seniors were asked to describe their grades in high school. The results appear in Table 33. High school seniors' self-reported grades increased slightly from 1972 to 1982 but still averaged about B-. Significant increases in grades are reported by males, high SES students, Whites, and students in the academic curriculum. In both 1972 and 1982, females, high SES students, Asian American students, students in Catholic schools, and students in the academic curriculum track reported higher grades than other students.

Table 33   Mean grades reported by high school seniors
(*Scale:* from 1 = below D to 8 = mostly A)

	1972	1982	Difference	Effect Size
Total	5.55	5.63	0.08*	0.05
Sex				
Male	5.26	5.37	0.11*	0.07
Female	5.84	5.89	0.05	0.04
SES				
Low	5.24	5.27	0.03	0.02
Middle	5.50	5.58	0.08	0.05
High	5.98	6.10	0.12*	0.09
Race/Ethnicity				
White	5.64	5.76	0.13*	0.09
Black	5.10	5.17	0.08	0.06
Mexican American	5.09	5.12	0.03	0.02
Puerto Rican	5.29	4.82	−0.47	−0.33
Other Hispanic	5.38	5.20	−0.14	−0.14
Asian American	5.99	6.01	0.02	0.01
American Indian	4.92	5.02	0.09	0.07
School Type				
Public	5.52	5.58	0.06	0.04
Private	5.58	6.06	0.48	0.38
Catholic	5.96	6.07	0.11	0.09
Curriculum				
Academic	6.05	6.30	0.25*	0.19
General	5.09	5.15	0.06	0.05
Vocational	5.20	5.30	0.10	0.08

* Statistically significant difference

In this table and the tables showing test score changes, we use effect size as well as simple differences. Effect size is the score change in standard deviation units. This allows comparison of changes without regard to the size of the samples.

There are two problems with this information about grades. First, because they are self-reports, we are less sure of their validity than we would be if we could use grade information from students' transcripts. (High school transcripts are available for the 1982 seniors. Comparisons between the transcripts and the self-reports suggest that there may be some tendency for students to over-report their grades.) Second, we do not know whether grades represent some absolute standard of accomplishment or if they are relative. Moreover, their value as indicators of educational attainment has been questioned by some, usually in association with evidence for 'grade inflation'. Consequently, a more absolute standard or common metric on which to evaluate educational attainment is needed. In NLS-72 and HS&B, this is done with achievement test results.

Table 34   Seniors' mean vocabulary test scores

	1972	1982	Difference	Effect Size
Total	6.55	5.76	−0.79*	−0.20
Sex				
Male	6.44	5.78	−0.66*	−0.17
Female	6.67	5.75	−0.92*	−0.23
SES				
Low	4.59	3.65	−0.94*	−0.28
Middle	6.52	5.64	−0.88*	−0.23
High	8.63	8.14	−0.49*	−0.13
Race/Ethnicity				
White	7.08	6.49	−0.58*	−0.15
Black	3.28	2.90	−0.39*	−0.13
Mexican American	3.47	3.19	−0.28	−0.09
Puerto Rican	3.80	3.25	−0.54	−0.17
Other Hispanic	4.64	4.14	−0.50	−0.14
Asian American	6.72	6.05	−0.67	−0.15
American Indian	4.04	3.56	−0.48	−0.14
School Type				
Public	6.44	5.50	−0.94*	−0.24
Private	7.88	8.53	0.65	0.15
Catholic	8.24	7.71	−0.53	−0.14
Curriculum				
Academic	8.29	8.02	−0.27*	−0.07
General	5.32	4.72	−0.59*	−0.17
Vocational	4.70	3.88	−0.82*	−0.25

* Statistically significant difference

Tested Achievement

The best evidence for use in determining the educational consequences of these changes in students, schools, and school experiences comes from three achievement tests, measuring vocabulary, reading, and mathematical skills and knowledge. Nine of the 15 vocabulary test items and 8 of the 20 reading test items were identical in 1972 and in 1982. The mathematics test was lengthened from 25 items in 1972 to 38 items in 1982; 18 of the original 1972 items were repeated on the 1982 mathematics test. To facilitate comparison of test scores, item response theory (IRT) equating was used to put the 1972 and 1982 test scores on a common scale. (See Rock *et al.*,[1] for details of this equating and a psychometric analysis of these tests.)

Changes in the achievement test scores across the decade are shown in Tables 34, 35 and 36.

Taken together, these three tables present a gloomy story. Scores declined on all three tests and for almost every subgroup from 1972 to 1982. There is a pattern evident in this decline. In every case, middle

Table 35 *Seniors' mean reading test scores*

	1972	1982	Difference	Effect Size
Total	9.89	8.13	−1.76*	−0.34
Sex				
Male	9.83	8.23	−1.60*	−0.31
Female	9.95	8.03	−1.92*	−0.38
SES				
Low	7.65	5.83	−1.82*	−0.39
Middle	9.92	8.06	−1.86*	−0.38
High	12.13	10.63	−1.51*	−0.31
Race/Ethnicity				
White	10.56	8.95	−1.61*	−0.33
Black	5.94	5.04	−0.90*	−0.21
Mexican American	6.28	5.25	−1.03*	−0.23
Puerto Rican	6.11	5.05	−1.06	−0.23
Other Hispanic	6.68	6.06	−0.61	−0.13
Asian American	10.14	8.36	−1.78	−0.33
American Indian	6.51	5.65	−0.86	−0.18
School Type				
Public	9.78	7.88	−1.90*	−0.37
Private	11.41	10.75	−0.66	−0.12
Catholic	11.61	10.09	−1.52*	−0.32
Curriculum				
Academic	11.99	10.86	−1.12*	−0.24
General	8.48	6.89	−1.59*	−0.34
Vocational	7.51	5.81	−1.70*	−0.38

* Statistically significant difference

Table 36 *Seniors' mean mathematics test scores*

	1972	1982	Difference	Effect Size
Total	12.94	11.43	−1.51*	−0.20
Sex				
Male	13.79	11.76	−2.30*	−0.27
Female	12.09	11.09	−1.00*	−0.14
SES				
Low	9.39	7.56	−1.24*	−0.27
Middle	12.90	11.29	−1.61*	−0.23
High	16.62	15.63	−0.99*	−0.15
Race/Ethnicity				
White	13.95	12.72	−1.24*	−0.17
Black	6.50	6.27	−0.23	−0.04
Mexican American	8.02	6.71	−1.31*	−0.20
Puerto Rican	6.33	6.41	0.07	0.01
Other Hispanic	8.04	8.39	0.36	0.05
Asian American	15.96	14.39	−1.58	−0.21
American Indian	7.74	7.26	−0.48	−0.08
School Type				
Public	12.79	11.00	−1.79*	−0.24
Private	15.50	15.29	−0.22	−0.03
Catholic	15.36	14.96	−0.40	−0.06
Curriculum				
Academic	16.66	16.05	−0.61*	−0.10
General	10.41	9.20	−1.21*	−0.18
Vocational	8.78	7.64	−1.15*	−0.18

* Statistically significant difference

and low SES students showed larger score declines than high SES students, students in the public schools had larger declines than students in non-public schools, and students in the general and vocational curricula showed greater declines than students in the academic curriculum. There appeared to be some convergence of test scores for females and males; the test score gap between White and minority students also narrowed somewhat.

In the next section, we try to untangle the reasons for these test score declines, separating the extent to which they are due to changes in the student populations, changes in the schools, and changes in students' school experiences.

Why Did the Test Scores Decline?

During the decade we have been discussing, there were other evidences of a decline in tested achievement, not only on the NLS-72 and HS&B achievement tests, but on other national tests as well. Similar score declines occurred in a selective college going population. The accompanying analysis based on the decline in the College Board (SAT) scores provides further evidence of the pervasiveness of the 'decline of the seventies'. That is, the decline was not limited to just a few students at lower ability levels but appears to have affected all levels.

Table 37 presents data on the extent of declines in tested achievement in reading and mathematics for two different tests involving different populations. The score decline figures are presented in standard deviation units for the 1972 and 1982 College Board SAT populations and for the NLS-72 and HS&B populations. By showing the decline in standard deviation units we can compare the relative extent of the declines across tests that are on different scales. For both populations the decline in terms of standard deviation units is greater in the verbal/reading area than in mathematics.

Educational experts are generally of two schools of thought concerning the probable reasons for the score decline of the seventies. One school of thought tends to explain the score decline in terms of population shifts. They argue that shifts in the high school population towards proportionately greater minority representation during the seventies could explain all or part of the score decline. This conclusion follows from the finding that minority and/or lower socioeconomic class students tend to perform less well on academic tests.

The second school of thought adheres to the view that the contribution of population shifts to the decline is minimal and the major

Table 37   Changes in SAT and NLS-HS&B test scores 1972–1982

SAT Test Score Changes, 1972 to 1982

	Verbal				Mathematics			
	1972	1982	Diff.	Change in SD Units	1972	1982	Diff.	Change in SD Units
Male	454	431	−23	−.21	505	493	−12	−.10
Female	452	421	−31	−.28	461	443	−18	−.16

NLS-HS&B Test Score Changes, 1972 to 1982

	Reading				Mathematics			
	1972	1982	Diff.	Change in SD Units	1972	1982	Diff.	Change in SD Units
Male	9.83	8.23	−1.60	−.31	13.79	11.76	−2.03	−.27
Female	9.95	8.03	−1.92	−.38	12.09	11.09	−1.00	−.14

culprits are changes in school standards and processes. The relative validity of these two competing hypothesis is examined in some detail in this chapter.

Methodology

Two statistical procedures are used to evaluate the comparative likelihood of the two competing hypotheses. The first procedure used is a 'population shift' partitioning of mean test score changes. The second method is an analysis of covariance partitioning of the test score changes.

The first method of partitioning takes the observed score decline in a particular tested area and partitions it into three components: (i) a population shift change; (ii) a within group mean change; and (iii) an interaction between the two. For example, the total population mean score decline might be a minus two score points from 1972 to 1982. This mean decline of two points can result from a decline in the means of certain subgroups and/or a change in the proportional representation of higher and lower scoring groups and their interaction.

The group mean change component (G) is estimated by calculating, for each subgroup, the subgroup's proportion in 1972, applying it to the subgroup's mean in the 1982 population, and then summing across all subgroups. The result is the mean score in 1982 that would have been expected if each subgroup's representation in the population had not changed but its mean had changed. The difference between this number and the observed 1972 mean is the change due to sub-group mean changes.

The change due to population shifts (P) is calculated by applying, for each subgroup, the group's proportion in the 1982 population to the group's mean score in 1972, and then summing over all sub-groups. The sum of G and P is generally not equal to the total mean change because of the interaction term (I). However, in almost all cases, the interaction is so small as to be considered negligible and not worth pursuing from the standpoint of interpretation.

The second methodological approach uses analysis of covariance to partition the total mean change (decline) into unique components associated with selected blocks of explanatory variables. These blocks parallel the groups of variables we have discussed thus far: demographics, the home educational support system, school characteristics, and students' educational experiences. This method complements the first, since it allows one to evaluate the impact of a block of explanatory variables on the test score decline while controlling for other confounding blocks of variables. The population shift methodology, on the other hand, is restricted to evaluating the impact of one or possibly two variables at a time.

Declines Attributable to Shifts in Populations

Changes in the size of various subpopulations in the two samples have been discussed earlier, primarily in Chapter 2. This showed that considerable demographic change occurred between 1972 and 1982 in the makeup of the high school senior population. Compared to 1972, the 1982 high school senior was more likely to be: (i) a member of a minority group; (ii) from the South; (iii) enrolled in a non-Catholic private school; and (iv) in a non-academic curriculum. While some of these shifts were relatively minor, there were considerable reductions in the proportion of the senior populations that were White or in the academic curriculum. As will be shown later, some of these shifts appear to be related to the test score decline.

Tables 38, 39 and 40 present the results of the population shift analysis separately for the NLS-HS&B vocabulary, reading, and mathematics test scores. The column labeled 'population shift' indicates the amount of decline in test score points that can be attributed to shifts in population from 1972 to 1982. The sign of the number indicates the direction of the effect of the population shift. For example, shifts in the population makeup (P) due to changes in race/

Table 38   Population shift effect, subgroup mean change effect, and change in moment* of grouping variables by IRT vocabulary score

Variables	Population Shift	Group Mean Change	Largest Change in Moment (percent)	Subgroup With Largest Change in Moment
Demographic				
Sex	.01	−.76	67	Females
SES	−.06	−.74	46	Middle
Race/Ethnicity	−.17	−.73	80	White students
Geographic region	−.06	−.79	32	South
Community type	−.09	−.88	55	Suburban
Student Behaviors				
Curriculum	−.25	−.58	52	Vocational, general
Hours of homework	−.12	−.66	85	Less than 5 hours
Educational plans	.00	−1.45	35	College
Semesters, mathematics	.14	−1.01	71	4 or fewer
Semesters, science	.02	−.88	91	4 or fewer
Semesters, language	−.07	−.78	71	3 or fewer
Athletic participation	.00	−.87	55	No participation
Attitude, academics	−.24	−.70	58	Disagree with more emphasis
School Characteristics				
Public, nonpublic	.02	−.92	92	Public
Projects used	−.06	−.79	57	Never, seldom
Essays used	−.01	−.83	57	Fairly often, frequently
Teachers ed.	.12	−.93	53	50–100% advanced
Percentage White	−.11	−.74	66	90–100%
Advanced placement	.12	−1.00	58	No advanced placement
Percentage, college	−.16	−.72	32	30–49%
Home Support				
Study aids	−.20	−.68	62	3 or more
Mother's aspirations	.10	−1.05	69	4-year college

* Moment refers to the extent to which a subgroup may have contributed to the total decline in comparison to the other subgroups of that variable.

ethnicity contributed a −0.17 of a score point to the overall vocabulary score change (see Table 38). This number can be compared to the 'subgroup mean change' in the same row (i.e., race/ethnicity). In this case the entry is −0.73 of a test score point indicating that the decline in racial/ethnic group means contributed considerably more to the overall mean decline than did population shifts in ethnic group makeup. The fourth column, 'subgroup with largest change', identifies which subgroup in each category contributed the most to the change. In the case of the race/ethnicity groups, the entry in this column and the third column indicate that 80 per cent of the population mean decline related to ethnicity could be attributed to declines within the White student population. This percentage reflects both the amount of the decline as well as the size of the groups involved.

Closer inspection of the Population Shift and Group Mean Change columns of Tables 38–40 suggest that, with some notable

Table 39   *Population shift effect, subgroup mean change effect, and change in moment* of grouping variables by IRT reading score*

Variables	Population Shift	Group Mean Change	Largest Change in Moment (percent)	Subgroup With Largest Change in Moment
Demographic				
Sex	.00	−.93	55	Females
SES	−.07	−.90	44	Middle
Race/Ethnicity	−.21	−.89	75	White students
Geographic region	−.05	−.99	40	South
Community type	−.06	−1.11	54	Suburban
Student Behaviors				
Curriculum	−.31	−.69	59	Vocational, general
Hours of homework	−.14	−.80	89	Less than 5 hours
Educational plans	−.01	−1.86	35	Vocational, Junior College
Semesters, mathematics	.19	−1.25	71	4 or fewer
Semesters, science	.02	−1.08	91	4 or fewer
Semesters, language	−.09	−.96	71	3 or fewer
Athletic participation	.03	−1.07	50	Yes, participates
Attitude, academics	−.30	−.83	58	Disagree with more emphasis
School Characteristics				
Public, nonpublic	.03	−1.12	92	Public
Projects used	−.07	−.96	62	Never, seldom
Essays used	−.02	−1.03	53	Fairly often, frequently
Teachers ed.	.12	−1.12	52	50–100% advanced
Percentage White	−.13	−.91	58	90–100%
Advanced placement	.12	−1.20	56	No advanced placement
Percentage, college	−.18	−.89	36	30–49%
Home Support				
Study aids	−.21	−.82	56	3 or more
Mother's aspirations	.12	−1.32	65	4-year college

* Moment refers to the extent to which a subgroup may have contributed to the total decline in comparison to the other subgroups of that variable.

exceptions, most of the decline can be attributed to mean score declines within populations and *not* to an increased representation in the population of traditionally low scoring groups.

The exceptions, where population shifts play a major role, include the relatively large movement of students from the academic curriculum to the vocational and general curricula. This shift had a particularly large negative impact on the mathematics test score.

It is interesting to note that the decline on all three tests is proportionately greater for lower and middle class students, White students, students in the South, and students living in urban areas. Black students showed less decline than White students while Mexican Americans exhibited declines similar to White students. It is also interesting to note that while girls showed bigger declines than boys on the verbal (reading and vocabulary) tests, the girls showed significantly less decline as compared to boys in mathematics.

Table 40 *Population shift effect, subgroup mean change effect, and change in moment* of grouping variables by IRT Mathematics score*

Variables	Population Shift	Group Mean Change	Largest Change in Moment (percent)	Subgroup With Largest Change in Moment
Demographic				
Sex	−.04	−.83	55	Male
SES	−.11	−.81	39	Middle
Race/Ethnicity	−.34	−.81	74	White students
Geographic region	−.08	−.91	59	South
Community type	−.07	−1.09	51	Suburban
Student Behaviors				
Curriculum	−.53	−.45	51	Vocational, general
Hours of homework	−.25	−.59	99	Less than 5 hours
Educational plans	−.09	−2.21	38	College
Semesters, mathematics	.44	−1.73	91	4 or fewer
Semesters, science	.05	−1.10	101	4 or fewer
Semesters, language	−.13	−.90	72	3 or fewer
Athletic participation	.14	−1.15	58	Yes, participates
School Characteristics				
Public, nonpublic	.04	−1.15	97	Public
Projects used	−.11	−.89	68	Never, seldom
Essays used	−.02	−.99	56	Never, seldom
Teachers ed.	.16	−1.19	51	0–49% advanced
Percentage White	−.20	−.80	59	90–100%
Advanced placement	.22	−1.32	61	No advanced placement
Percentage, college	−.29	−.77	32	30–49%
Home Support				
Study aids	−.34	−.68	50	2 or fewer
Mother's aspirations	.21	−1.48	73	4-year college

* Moment refers to the extent to which a subgroup may have contributed to the total decline in comparison to the other subgroups of that variable.

As indicated earlier, the differential in favor of boys with respect to the number of mathematics courses taken was significantly reduced during the seventies.

In summary, the population shift analysis suggests that changes in population demographics played a small role in the observed score decline in any of the three tested areas. Shifts towards an increase in the number of students matriculating in the general and vocational programs did contribute significantly to the score decline.

Relationship Between Student and School Processes and Test Score Decline

As indicated above, the population shift analysis cross-classifies populations across only one dimension at a time. This does not allow examination of the effects on score decline of population shifts while controlling for the effects of numerous other confounding variables. This section evaluates the impact of selected blocks of variables on the 1972–1982 mean score changes after controlling for other confounding blocks. The four blocks of variables included in this analysis were:

> *Demographics:* sex, family SES, race/ethnicity, region of the country, and community type.
>
> *Home educational support system*: students' self-report of parental influence on plans, father's edutional level, mother's educational level, parents'/mothers' educational aspirations for students, and study aids available in the home.
>
> *School characteristics*: student self-reports yielding school means on quality of the physical plant, quality of the library, quality of the academic instruction, school reputation, teacher interest, amount of homework done, schools' emphasis on academics, labs in courses, essays in courses, and number of courses in various subject matter areas. School questionnaire data included per cent White, percent of teachers with an advanced degree, teacher turnover, student-teacher ratios, availability of bilingual education, and advanced placement courses.
>
> *Student educational experiences*: curriculum track, semesters in selected subject matter areas, amount of homework, athletic participation, academic attitudes, and educational plans.

The procedure used here was a 'step down' analysis of covariance, where the primary outcome is the difference between covariate adjusted means when a particular block is left out of the analysis. To arrive at an estimate of the unique contribution of a given block to the 1972–1982 mean test score decline, one first compares the spread between adjusted means when all four blocks are controlled for (i.e. the full model); one then recomputes the adjusted means when the specified block is removed (a reduced model). If the assumptions of the analysis of covariance model are reasonably met, then the difference between the spread of the reduced model and that of the full model is an estimate of the block's relative influence on the mean decline while controlling for the other blocks. This partition also gives an indication of the direction of influence of each of the blocks. (In this case, positive numbers indicate blocks of variables that contribute to the decline; negative numbers indicate blocks of variables that work against, or resist, score decline.)

Figure 1 presents estimates of the relative contribution of each of the blocks to the score decline in vocabulary, reading, and mathema-

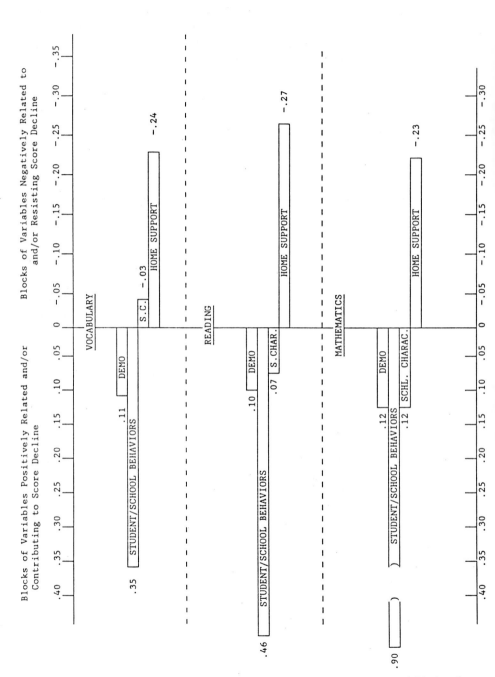

Figure 1: Adjusted mean differences for 1972–1982 test scores by selected blocks of explanatory variables

tics while controlling for the remaining blocks. The numbers on the bars indicate the unique contribution of that particular block to the overall score decline. For example, the student school experiences block contributes 0.35 of a test score point to the overall decline in vocabulary while the school characteristics block resists the decline somewhat (-0.03).

Changes between 1972 and 1982 in demographics contributed only 0.10 to 0.12 of a score point decline. The negative numbers on the bar associated with the home educational support system for all three tested areas indicates that change between 1972 and 1982 in variables that make up this block were in a direction of resisting score decline (contributing to a test score increase). In the case of vocabulary, if there had been no change in home educational support between 1972 and 1982, the expected score decline would have been .24 of a score point greater.

Inspection of Figure 1 indicates that the primary contributor to the score decline in all tested areas was students' school experiences. In all cases demographics and school characteristics contributed comparatively little to the score decline when contrasted with the 1972–1982 changes in school experiences. As in most analyses of this type, the impact of the school characteristics tends to be biassed downward because of the relatively high correlations with the students' school experiences. Many measures at the school level are aggregate scores of individual level variables, such as number of mathematics courses, foreign language courses, etc. It is nearly impossible to separate students' school experiences from school processes, rules and requirements.

Within each block certain variables were identified that contributed most to the score decline. Changes in individual student educational experiences from 1972–1982 that contributed the most to score decline were:

- Taking fewer semesters of foreign language courses. This reduction was proportionately greater for females.
- Spending less time on homework. This reduction was proportionately greater for females.
- Taking fewer semesters of science courses.
- Not being in the academic curriculum.

Changes from 1972–1982 in individual school characteristics that contributed most to the test score decline were:

- An increase in the proportion of students rating the school as needing more academic emphasis.

- A decrease in the amount of homework done by students.
- A decrease in school means with respect to semesters of foreign language courses taken by students.
- An increase in schools with a high dropout rate.
- A decrease in school means with respect to laboratory courses taken by students.
- A decrease in students' ratings of their school's reputation in the community.
- A decrease in the students' ratings of the quality of their academic instruction.
- A decrease in students' rating of the physical condition of their school buildings.

The only significant variable in the demographic block was being White.

The results of the analysis of covariance partition agree fairly well with those of the population shift analysis. Both methods suggest that population shifts, in particular increased representation of minority groups, had little to do with the score decline of the seventies. The primary culprits in the score decline were changes that took place in both student school experiences and in school processes.

This is not to say that changes during the seventies in the direction of increased heterogeneity of the student population might not have had an indirect effect on school processes which in turn affected the rate of score decline. Rightly or wrongly, school administrators and legislators may have believed that the changes in the ethnic makeup of their student bodies that occurred during these years required adjustments in both the educational services as well as educational standards. Certain special reading and mathematics programs, including Title 1 programs and, bilingual programs, were initiated during these years. It would appear that these programs were effective in the sense that the predominant consumers of these programs (low SES Blacks and Hispanics) showed proportionately less decline than the White middle class student. However, special programs that target special subpopulations may use up the limited educational resources available within any one school system. This reallocation of resources may be at the expense of the remaining nontargeted student population.

Summary

Although there was a slight rise, from 1972 to 1982, in the average grades reported by high school seniors, achievement test scores for this same period showed significant declines. Two competing hypothesis about potential causes of the score decline among high school seniors during the seventies were investigated. The first hypothesis argues that increased numbers of minority group members, many of whom are traditionally characterized as low achieving students, was the primary reason for the observed score decline. The second hypothesis is less specific. It suggests that population shifts played a minor role in the score decline, and that changes in students' school experiences and in school processes were the major factors behind the score decline.

Two independent methodologies were used to evaluate the relative validity of the two hypotheses. Both methods suggested that the score declines in vocabularly, reading, and mathematics were primarily due to changes in students' school experiences and to changes in school processes that occurred during the seventies. Change in student population demographics that occurred during these years accounted for 15 to 25 per cent of the score decline.

Note

1. Rock, D. A., Hilton, T. L., Pollack, J., Ekstrom R. B. and Goertz, M. E. (1985) *Psychometric Analysis of the NLS and the High School and Beyond Test Batteries.* NCES 85-218. Washington, DC: US Government Printing Office.

PART 3
ACHIEVEMENT AND PERSISTENCE
IN HIGH SCHOOL: A CLOSER LOOK

Introduction

The preceding section of this book compares high school seniors and their schools across a decade of time. This comparison, while informative, does not provide information about how these differences in educational status may have arisen. We wonder, for example, if the increase in high school dropouts between 1972 and 1982 may, in part, account for some of the observed differences in the two groups of seniors. We also wonder how students' educational experiences before their senior year in high school contribute to the characteristics we observed in the senior year.

In this section we will explore how the students who were 'on track' to be become seniors in 1982 developed during their last two years of high school. In Chapter 6 we identify the school and student behavior processes that facilitate intellectual growth during the last two years of high school. In Chapter 7 we look at persistence in the final two years of high school. We compare those students who became dropouts with those students who persisted in high school. We try to answer the questions 'Who drops out of high school and why? and 'Does persisting in high school result in higher achievement?'

6   What Determines Achievement Growth in High School?

We have spent considerable time comparing two groups of high school seniors. We have found that similar factors — background, family educational support, students' school experiences, and school characteristics and processes — explain the achievement of the individuals in each group. We have seen how changes in these factors explain the decline in tested achievement that occurred between 1972 and 1982.

We now turn to the problem of understanding how the students developed during their high school years to become the kinds of individuals we have observed as seniors. To do this, we use longitudinal data. This part of the HS&B data collection began when these students were high school sophomores in 1980. At that time a base-year survey and tests in vocabulary, reading, mathematics, science and writing were administered to about 30,000 students in over 1,000 public and private schools. A follow-up survey collected data from and retested over 22,000 of these students who were seniors in 1982.

How Did These Students Change Between Their Sophomore and Senior Years?

In this section, we will look briefly at changes in the students during their last two years of high school. These changes related primarily to behaviors, attitudes, plans and tested achievement. There is, in addition, information about family background that was not included in the earlier analysis because no comparable information was available for the 1972 cohort.

Family Structure

One important piece of background information has to do with family structure. Coleman and Hoffer have used the term 'deficient families'; they say '[T]he two principal indicators of structural deficiency ... are single-parent households and working mothers'.[1] These authors argue that deficient family structure is associated with low achievement in high school and with high school attrition.

In 1980, approximately 71 per cent of the HS&B sophomores indicated they lived with both natural parents, 9 per cent with one natural parent and a step-parent, 15 per cent with the mother only, and about one per cent each with father only or with grandparents. These percentages varied, however, across subgroups. Slightly more than half (approximately 53 per cent) of all of Black high school sophomores did not live in households where both parents were present. Similar data reported by the Bureau of the Census indicate that 52 per cent of all Black families were one parent households. More than 40 per cent of low SES students also lived in households where both natural parents were not present.

Educational Aspirations

There was, somewhat surprisingly, no change in the overall educational aspirations for students who remained in high school between the sophomore and senior years. At both points in time, approximately 57 per cent of students indicated they intended to enroll in some form of postsecondary education. However, there were some shifts in the type of schooling these students planned on obtaining. The major change was a decline (−4.21 per cent) in students planning to enter a four-year college or university and a corresponding rise in students planning to enter two-year colleges or vocational/technical schools.

Self-concept

Students who stayed in high school improved in self-concept between their sophomore and senior years. There were significant shifts toward more positive self-concept on all self-concept scale items in the student surveys. There were also indications of improved self-concept in students' responses to other survey questions. For example, 78 per cent the students indicated, as sophomores, and 84 per cent as seniors, that they were popular with other students. Eighty three per cent of the sophomores and 89 per cent of the seniors said others thought of them as attractive.

Locus of Control

Students also changed, between their sophomore and senior years, in their sense of control over their lives. There were significant changes, in the direction of more internalized control, on all items on the locus of control scale.

Other Attitudes

There was a slight decline in the students' interest in school between their sophomore and senior years. Seventy five per cent of the seniors, as compared to 79 per cent of the sophomores, said they found school interesting. The decreasing interest in school was greater among males than females, among middle and high SES students, and among students in the general curriculum.

The students were also asked about their interest in specific school subjects. Only about a third of the students indicated that they found their English or their mathematics courses interesting. This level of interest (or disinterest) did not change between the sophomore and senior years.

School Behavior

There were more attendance problems among these students as seniors than as sophomores. This included increases in the number of days the students were absent for reasons other than illness, in the percentage of students who cut classes (24 per cent of the sophomores, 39 per cent of the seniors), and in the number of days the students were tardy. By their senior year, approximately 12 per cent of the students reported having been suspended or put on probation. However, more minor problems, such as coming to class unprepared or without homework done, decreased as the students matured. About 13 per cent of the seniors, as contrasted with 15 per cent of the sophomores, reported having disciplinary problems in the previous school year.

In-school and Out-of-school Activities

The students participated less in most extra-curricular school activities as seniors than they had done as sophomores. The major exception was vocational education clubs, which showed a ten percent increase in participation rates. There was also a small, but statistically significant, decrease in the amount of time spent on homework by the

Table 41 *Mean vocabulary test scores and gains from sophomore to senior year*

	Sophomore	Senior	Difference	Effect Size
Total	9.02	11.17	2.2*	0.4
Sex				
Male	9.23	11.24	2.0*	0.4
Female	8.82	11.11	2.3*	0.4
SES				
Low	6.11	8.09	2.0*	0.4
Middle	9.04	11.19	2.2*	0.4
High	11.82	14.15	2.3*	0.5
Race/Ethnicity				
White	10.03	12.24	2.2*	0.4
Black	4.58	6.50	1.9*	0.4
Mexican American	5.55	7.14	1.6*	0.3
Puerto Rican	5.36	7.47	2.1*	0.4
Other Hispanic	7.03	9.32	2.3*	0.4
Asian American	9.05	11.39	2.3*	0.4
American Indian	6.30	8.43	2.1*	0.4
School Type				
Public	8.76	10.87	2.1*	0.4
Private	11.82	14.48	2.7*	0.5
Catholic	11.28	13.79	2.5*	0.5
Curriculum				
Academic	11.65	14.07	2.4*	0.5
General	7.75	9.81	2.1*	0.4
Vocational	6.63	8.48	1.9*	0.4

* Statistically significant difference

students as seniors, as compared to the amount of homework they had done as sophomores. One possible reason for these declines may be increased participation in paid work. Only about 42 per cent of the sophomores indicated they were involved in paid work but, by their senior year, 64 per cent of these students had a paid job. The typical sophomore reported working about nine hours a week, while the typical senior was employed for 16 hours a week. Television watching declined from about three hours per day for sophomores to about two hours a day for seniors. Not surprisingly, the students spent more time as seniors than they had as sophomores in dating, talking with friends, and riding around.

Grades and Tested Achievement

The students who remained in high school showed a slight, but statistically significant, increase in grades from their sophomore to their senior year. The typical grade, at both times, was about a B−.

Students who remained in high school made significant gains in all areas of tested achievement between their sophomore and senior years. These gains are shown in Tables 41–45.

Table 42   Mean reading test scores and gains from sophomore to senior year

	Sophomore	Senior	Difference	Effect Size
Total	7.16	8.54	1.4*	0.3
Sex				
Male	7.27	8.66	1.4*	0.3
Female	7.06	8.42	1.4*	0.3
SES				
Low	5.03	6.31	1.3*	0.3
Middle	7.11	8.48	1.4*	0.3
High	9.34	10.89	1.5*	0.3
Race/Ethnicity				
White	7.89	9.29	1.4*	0.3
Black	4.21	5.36	1.1*	0.3
Mexican American	4.35	5.62	1.3*	0.3
Puerto Rican	4.45	5.77	1.3	0.3
Other Hispanic	5.08	6.86	1.8*	0.4
Asian American	7.52	9.10	1.6*	0.3
American Indian	4.95	6.24	1.3	0.3
School Type				
Public	6.99	8.33	1.3*	0.3
Private	8.93	10.91	2.0*	0.4
Catholic	8.71	10.37	1.7*	0.4
Curriculum				
Academic	9.50	11.11	1.6*	0.3
General	5.97	7.29	1.3*	0.3
Vocational	5.10	6.20	1.1*	0.3

* Statistically significant difference

Table 43   Mean mathematics test scores and gains from sophomore to senior year

	Sophomore	Senior	Difference	Effect Size
Total	13.43	15.43	2.0*	0.2
Sex				
Male	13.86	16.13	2.3*	0.2
Female	13.01	14.73	1.7*	0.2
SES				
Low	8.47	9.74	1.3*	0.1
Middle	13.36	15.26	1.9*	0.2
High	18.41	21.23	2.8*	0.3
Race/Ethnicity				
White	15.10	17.16	2.1*	0.2
Black	6.04	7.91	1.9*	0.2
Mexican American	7.59	8.67	1.1	0.1
Puerto Rican	6.02	7.65	1.6	0.2
Other Hispanic	9.56	11.49	1.9*	0.2
Asian American	17.94	20.88	2.9	0.3
American Indian	8.17	9.25	1.1	0.1
School Type				
Public	12.99	14.87	1.9*	0.2
Private	18.55	20.91	2.4*	0.2
Catholic	17.07	20.32	3.2*	0.4
Curriculum				
Academic	18.70	21.97	3.3*	0.3
General	10.55	11.99	1.4*	0.2
Vocational	8.99	9.69	0.7*	0.1

* Statistically significant difference

Table 44   Mean science test scores and gains from sophomore to senior year

	Sophomore	Senior	Difference	Effect Size
Total	9.27	10.23	1.0*	0.2
Sex				
Male	9.94	10.95	1.0*	0.2
Female	8.60	9.51	0.9*	0.2
SES				
Low	7.03	7.90	0.9*	0.2
Middle	9.36	10.36	1.0*	0.2
High	11.34	12.28	0.9*	0.2
Race/Ethnicity				
White	10.17	11.12	0.9*	0.2
Black	5.20	6.10	0.9*	0.2
Mexican American	6.36	7.29	0.9*	0.2
Puerto Rican	5.75	7.31	1.6*	0.3
Other Hispanic	7.47	8.52	1.1*	0.2
Asian American	9.36	11.05	1.7*	0.4
American Indian	7.11	7.95	0.8*	0.2
School Type				
Public	9.14	10.08	0.9*	0.2
Private	11.05	11.84	0.8	0.2
Catholic	10.24	11.41	1.2*	0.3
Curriculum				
Academic	11.17	12.15	1.1*	0.3
General	8.37	9.28	0.9*	0.2
Vocational	7.49	8.31	0.8*	0.2

* Statistically significant difference

Table 45   Mean writing test scores and gains from sophomore to senior year

	Sophomore	Senior	Difference	Effect Size
Total	8.92	10.61	1.7*	0.3
Sex				
Male	7.78	9.42	1.6*	0.3
Female	10.06	11.79	1.7*	0.4
SES				
Low	6.82	8.57	1.7*	0.4
Middle	8.96	10.64	1.7*	0.4
High	10.99	12.61	1.6*	0.4
Race/Ethnicity				
White	9.69	11.33	1.6*	0.4
Black	5.58	7.36	1.8*	0.4
Mexican American	6.08	7.86	1.8*	0.4
Puerto Rican	5.08	8.10	3.0*	0.7
Other Hispanic	6.63	8.66	2.0*	0.4
Asian American	10.33	12.03	1.7*	0.4
American Indian	6.41	8.08	1.7	0.3
School Type				
Public	8.71	10.39	1.7*	0.3
Private	10.57	12.37	1.8*	0.4
Catholic	10.89	12.63	1.7*	0.4
Curriculum				
Academic	11.21	12.87	1.7*	0.4
General	7.73	9.44	1.7*	0.4
Vocational	6.89	8.58	1.7*	0.3

* Statistically significant difference

Gains in vocabulary between the sophomore and senior years were greater for high SES students, students in non-public schools, and students in the academic curriculum. Gains in reading were greatest among students in non-public schools. High SES students, Asian American students, Catholic school students, and students in the academic curriculum made the greatest gains in mathematics. Asian American and Puerto Rican students made the greatest gains in science while Puerto Rican students made the greatest gains in writing.

The tables also include information about the test score gains in pretest standard deviation units (effect size) for various subgroups within the total population. Presenting the gains this way allows one to compare the relative size of the gains across tests of differing lengths and without regard to the size of the subgroup. Inspection of the gains indicates that there are relatively larger gains in the verbal areas (vocabulary and reading) than in the mathematics and science areas. It would appear that greater gains are found in those skills which can be learned outside of school as well as in school.

How Can We Explain These Gains?

In Chapter 5 we argued, hopefully persuasively, that the decline in tested achievement that took place between 1972 and 1982 was due primarily to changes in students' school experiences and in their schools and, to a lesser degree, to population shifts. While the evidence for those conclusions was based on the application of relatively comprehensive and sophisticated statistical methodology to two large national probability samples, the fact remains that the samples are cross-sectional.

It is well known that in any cross-sectional comparison there may be generational differences in the two cohorts that may not be appropriately measured and/or statistically controlled. We, in fact, have documented in some detail in Chapter 2 differences in the two cohorts, for example, in racial/ethnic composition. In the partitioning analysis in Chapter 5, we took steps to control for the potential impact that this difference may have on our conclusions. This does not, however, mean there may not be other important variables that differentiate the two cohorts but remain unmeasured and thus are not available for statistical control. Our primary finding, that the decline in achievement was due to changes in student learning experiences, needs additional support from data that are more appropriate for inferring cause and effect.

Specifically, we would like to see whether the same factors that played a key role in explaining the decline in tested achievement between 1972 and 1982 will also explain achievement gains during the last two years of high school. We use the longitudinal data on those HS&B students who were high school sophomores in 1980 and seniors in 1982 to make this test.

Longitudinal data bases measure the same people at two or more points in time and thus are less subject to the confounding of generational and cohort differences with changes in achievement over time. If we can show that the same student/school variables that were related to score declines in the cross-sectional study are also related to differential gains in achievement in a national longitudinal study, then our cause and effect argument becomes much stronger.

Fortunately, virtually all of the variables that were used in the cross-sectional study were also used when the HS&B cohort was first tested as sophomores in 1980; most variables that were amenable to change were also assessed again in 1982 when these students were seniors. The availability of student and school process variables, along with tested achievement at both the sophomore and senior year, enables us to relate the observed gains in tested achievement to variations in student learning experiences and school processes that took place during the last two years of high school. Our general model for this analysis is shown in Figure 2.

Determinants of Achievement Gains

What explains achievement gains in high school? Inspection of the total column of Tables 46–50 shows that two variables had consistently large direct effects on gains in test scores between the sophomore and senior years on all five achievement tests for the total group of students. These variable are:

- Number of relevant courses (eg., number of language courses for vocabulary, reading and writing achievement; number of mathematics courses; for mathematics achievement; and number of science courses for science achievement) taken between the sophomore and senior years; and
- Amount of homework done.

The next question is 'Do these, and the other major variables, have similar effects for students of all racial/ethnic groups?'

Even if the same variables explain gains in tested achievement for

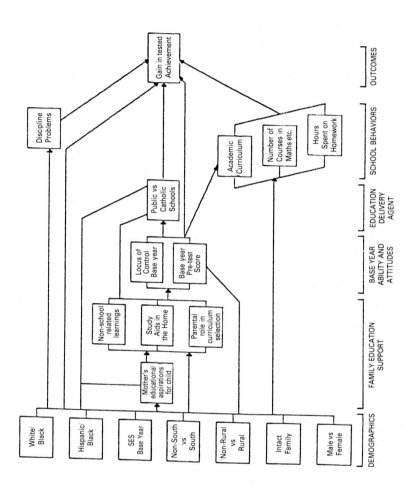

Figure 2: Explanatory Model for Achievement Gains

the total group of students, the question remains. How generalizable are these gains? Do the same educational processes work in the same way for majority and minority students?

In Tables 46–50 we present the determinants of achievement (standardized regression weights) for each of the five tests separately for the total group of students and for three racial/ethnic groups — Whites, Blacks, and Hispanics (Mexican Americans and Puerto Ricans). Instead of using race/ethnicity as a background variable, we use White and Hispanic separately to contrast gains made by students from these groups with gains made by Black students. In these analyses the sophomore year (pretest) score is used as a control variable for initial status. Score gain differences, where presented, are based on the raw regression weights (See Rock *et al.*[2] for the raw regression weight tables). The asterisks indicate significant regression weights. We use a t-statistic of 4 rather than 2 because the sampling plan is half as efficient as a true random sample.

Determinants of Gains in Vocabulary

For the total group, the two largest determinants of gain in vocabulary are race/ethnicity and the number of language courses taken. Whites gained 0.9 of a score point more than Blacks. Although the number of foreign language courses taken is a significant determinant of vocabulary for Whites and Blacks, it is not a major determinant for Hispanics, suggesting that it is the exposure to another language which facilitates vocabulary development among language majority students. Students who had an internalized locus of control, that is, those who felt they could control their futures, gained more than students with externalized control, or a sense of powerlessness. Students whose parents had high educational aspirations for them gained more than students whose parents had lower aspirations for their children. White and Hispanic students from higher SES backgrounds gained more than similar students from lower SES backgrounds. Students who did more homework gained more than those who did less homework. Students whose families provided more non-school opportunities for learning gained more than students who did not have these opportunities.

Determinants of Gains in Reading

The largest determinant of gains in reading for the total group is the number of language courses taken. Students with internalized locus of

Table 46   Major determinants of senior year vocabulary score for total group and for three racial/ethnic groups
(Standardized regession weights)

	Total	White	Black	Hispanic
Background				
Sex	.01	.00	.04	.00
SES	.03*	.04*	−.03	.04
White	.06*			
Hispanic	.00			
Region	.01	.01	.01	.06
Family Support				
Parents' Aspirations	.03*	.02	.04	.09*
Non-school Learning	.02*	.02	.02	.04
Study Aids	.01	.00	.02	.02
Sophomore Year				
Ability & Attitudes				
Vocabulary Test Score	.51*	.52*	.49*	.50*
Locus of Control	.04*	.03*	.05*	.06
School Characteristics				
Public	−.00	−.01	−.00	−.02
Percentage College-Bound	.00	.01	.01	−.02
Student Experiences				
Curriculum	.01	.01	.01	−.01
Number of Language Courses	.06*	.06*	.09*	−.00
Homework	.02*	.02	.00	.05
Disciplinary Problems	−.01	−.01	−0.4	−.03

* Variables whose associated raw weights are at least four times their standard error.

Table 47   Major determinants of senior year reading test score for total group and three racial/ethnic groups
(Standardized regression weights)

	Total	White	Black	Hispanic
Background				
Sex	.03*	.02	.06	.03
SES	.00	.01	−.00	−.05
White	−.00			
Hispanic	−.00			
Region	−.02	−.02*	−.02	.00
Family Support				
Parents' Aspirations	.02	.01	.04	.14*
Non-school Learning	.01	.02	−.00	−.00
Study Aids	−.01	−.01	·−.01	.01
Sophomore Year				
Ability & Attitudes				
Reading Test Score	.34*	.35*	.33*	.28*
Locus of Control	.03*	.03*	.06	.04
School Characteristics				
Public	−.01	−.01	−.01	−.00
Percentage College-Bound	−.01	−.02	.01	−.01
Student Experiences				
Curriculum	.01	.01	.02	−.05
Number of Language Courses	.05*	.05*	.07	.03
Homework	.03*	.04*	.02	−.00
Disciplinary Problems	−.01	−.01	−.02	−.03

* Variables whose associated raw weights are at least four times their standard error.

Education and American Youth

Table 48   Major determinants of senior year mathematics test score for total group and three
racial/ethnic groups
(Standardized regression weights)

	Total	White	Black	Hispanic
Background				
Sex	.04*	.05*	.06*	.03
SES	.02*	.02*	.01	.02
White	.02*			
Hispanic	−.01			
Region	.02*	.03*	.01	.04
Family Support				
Parents' Aspirations	.03*	.03*	.01	.03
Non-school Learning	.01	.01	−.01	.00
Study Aids	−.01	−.01	.00	−.01
Sophomore Year				
Ability & Attitudes				
Mathematics Test Score	.53*	.53*	.49*	.46*
Locus of Control	.00	−.00	.01	.02
School Characteristics				
Public	.03*	.03*	.03	⁻ ⁼
Percentage College-Bound	.02*	.02	.03	.03
Student Experiences				
Curriculum	.02*	.02	.02	.01
Number of Math Courses	.22*	.23*	.24*	.26*
Homework	.04*	.04*	.06*	.06*
Disciplinary Problems	−.02*	−.02	−.03	−.03

* Variables whose associated raw weights are at least four times their standard errors.

Table 49   Major determinants of senior year science test score for total group and three
racial/ethnic groups
(Standardized regression weight)

	Total	White	Black	Hispanic
Background				
Sex	.09*	.10*	.11*	.10*
SES	.02	.03	−.02	.02
White	.09*			
Hispanic	.03*			
Region	.03*	.02*	.05	.11*
Family Support				
Parents' Aspirations	.02	.02	.00	.07
Non-school Learning	.02*	.02	.02	.02
Study Aids	−.00	−.00	.00	−.00
Sophomore Year				
Ability & Attitudes				
Science Test Score	.43*	.43*	.45*	.39*
Locus of Control	.02	.02	.03	.00
School Characteristics				
Public	−.00	−.00	.01	.04
Percentage College-Bound	−.02*	−.03*	.02	−.02
Student Experiences				
Curriculum	−.01	−.01	.01	−.05
Number of Science Courses	.05*	.05*	.05	.12*
Homework	.02*	.02	.05	.06
Disciplinary Problems	−.02*	−.03*	−.02	.01

* Variables whose associated raw weights are at least four times their standard error.

Table 50   Major determinants of senior year writing test score for total group and three racial/ethnic groups
(Standardized regression weights)

	Total	White	Black	Hispanic
Background				
Sex	−.15*	−.16*	−.14*	−.17*
SES	−.02	−.01	−.02	−.03
White	.04*			
Hispanic	.02			
Region	−.00	−.01	−.03	.06
Family Support				
Parents' Aspirations	.04*	.04*	.03	.07
Non-school Learning	.02	.01	.02	.03
Study Aids	.03*	.02	.04	.03
Sophomore Year				
Ability & Attitudes				
Writing Test Score	.37*	.37*	.37*	.27*
Locus of Control	.02*	.02	.02	.03
School Characteristics				
Public	−.00	−.01	.00	−.01
Percentage College-Bound	−.00	−.00	.03	−.02
Student Experiences				
Curriculum	−.00	−.01	.02	.01
Number of Language Courses	.04*	.05*	.04	.03
Homework	.05*	.04*	.06*	.06
Disciplinary Problems	−.05*	−.05*	−.06*	−.08*

* Variables whose associated raw weights are at least four times their standard error.

control gained more than students with an externalized sense of control. The amount of homework done was also an important determinant for White and, to a lesser extent, Black students (but not for Hispanic students). Males gained approximately 0.25 of a score point more than females. Whites in the South gained more than their counterparts in other regions of the country. Hispanic students whose parents had high educational aspirations for them gained about 0.5 a score point more than Hispanic students whose parents had lower aspirations for their children.

Determinants of Gains in Mathematics

The number of mathematics courses taken by students were, by far, the major determinants of gains in mathematics achievement. Sex is the next largest determinant; males gained approximately 1.0 score points more than females. (Hispanic males had somewhat less advantage.) The amount of homework done was also a major determinant. Attending a public school led to larger test score gains in mathematics, although this effect was less strong for Hispanic students. Parents' educational aspirations had a major effect on gains in mathematics for

Whites and Hispanics, but not for Blacks. White and Hispanic students from the South gained less than their counterparts from other areas of the country. High SES White students gained more than low SES White students. Both Black and White students in the academic curriculum made larger gains than their classmates in other curricula. Students who did not have disciplinary problems gained more than students who had these problems.

Later on in this chapter we will present more information on the 'mechanics' of gains in mathematics skills. This will allow us to see if these gains are unique to specific mathematical operations or skill levels or if they occur across the board. For example, gains in mathematics scores might be primarily related to gains in simple arithmatic operations but not simple algebraic manipulations or *vice-versa*. Conversely, the gain may be permeating all mathematical skill levels. Evidence of a differential gain, that is, again specific to one or more skill levels, may point the way to parts of the mathematics curriculum needing special attention.

Determinants of gains in science

The largest gains in science achievement were associated with being male; male students gained, on average, 0.85 more score points than females. The number of science courses taken was the second largest determinant of achievement gains in this area. Students from the South gained less than students from other regions of the country; the negative effect of residing in the South was much greater for Hispanics than for Whites or Blacks.

Determinants of gains in writing

In contrast to gains in mathematics and science, gains in writing were associated with being female. Females gained approximately 1.5 score points more than males on this test. Three student experience variables also showed major relationships with gains in writing. Students who had fewer disciplinary problems, who took more language courses, and who did more homework all had larger score gains than students who did not exhibit these behaviors. Students whose parents had high educational aspirations for them gained more than students whose parents had lower aspirations; this was especially true for Hispanic students. The number of study aids in the home was also related to gains on the writing achievement test (perhaps this is an area where having a dictionary and a typewriter makes a real difference).

Students with an internalized locus of control gained more than students with an externalized sense of control.

Relative Adjusted Gains in Achievement

The relative adjusted gains in achievement for males and females and for the major racial/ethnic groups need to be put into perspective. The group contrasts, in terms of pre-test standard deviation units, are shown in Table 51. It should be kept in mind that these group comparisons in adjusted means are, essentially, answering the question 'What would be the expected gains if one compared the students in these groups who had the same background characteristics and family support, who had the same sophomore year achievement test scores and attitudes, who attended schools with the same characteristics, and who had the same educational experiences (eg., were in the same curriculum, took the same courses, did the same amount of homework)? These comparisons show that there would be relatively little difference in the achievement of majority and minority students in reading, mathematics, and writing under these conditions. We consider group differences of 10 per cent of a standard deviation or greater as being 'practically significant'. The advantage of Whites in vocabulary and in science likely results from variables unmeasured in this study — for example, classroom interaction processes. The comparison also shows that, all of the major factors of this study being equal, there would be little difference in the gains in tested achievement of males and females in vocabulary, reading and mathematics but that differences in science and writing achievement gains would probably remain.

The above analysis indicates that students' school experiences are the primary determinants of gains in tested achievement, regardless of race/ethnicity or sex. The number of relevant courses taken, being in the academic curriculum, the amount of homework done, and not having disciplinary problems are the major determinants of gain. In the next section we will see what background and home support factors contribute to students having these facilitating experiences.

Factors Contributing to Students' Educational Experiences

We would like to know to what extent background and family support factors contribute to students having these facilitating educational experiences in high school. This information not only helps us to

Table 51   *Relative adjusted achievement gains in standard deviation units*

	Vocab.	Read.	Math.	Sci.	Writing
Whites in comparison to:					
Blacks	+.17	100	+.06	+.25	+.11
Hispanics	+.16	+.02	+.09	+.12	+.04
Males in comparison to:					
Females	+.02	+.05	+.10	+.19	−.29

model the relationship between home experiences, school experiences, and student achievement, but also provides practical information for families who wish to have their children succeed in school. The following section discusses the determinants of various student school experience variables that have already been shown to be related to achievement gains.

Course-taking

The number of courses students take in language, mathematics and science are all primarily determined by sophomore achievement and by being in the academic curriculum (See Table 52). Students in the academic curriculum took approximately half a year more of mathematics and of science and three-quarters of a year more of language than comparable students in other curricula. Students in public schools took about one less course in mathematics and in foreign languages than students in non-public schools; however, public school students took slightly more course work in science. The other major determinants of course-taking were parents' educational aspirations for the student and not having disciplinary problems.

Curriculum

Students who had high scores on the sophomore year vocabulary test and who had parents with high educational aspirations for them were most likely to be in the academic curriculum (See Table 53). Attending a non-public high school also increased the probability of a student being in the academic curriculum, as did having parents who were involved in helping the student plan her/his high school program.

Homework

Students who did more homework were those who took more courses in mathematics and in languages and who were not disciplinary problems (See Table 54). Females did more homework than males. Students whose parents had been involved in helping them

Table 52   Major determinants of number of courses taken for total group
(Standardized regression weights)

	Mathematics	Science	Language
Background			
Sex	.03*	.07*	−.12*
SES	.03*	−.00	.08
Race/ethnicity	−.02	−.05*	−.06*
Region	−.05*	−.08*	.08*
Community	.03*	−.01	.06*
Family Support			
Parents' Aspirations	.11*	.11*	.10*
Non-school Learning	.03*	−.01	.07*
Study Aids	.02	.02	−.01
Intact Family	.01	.02	.00
Parental Role in Program Planning	.01	.01	.01
Sophomore Year			
Ability & Attitudes			
Sophomore Achievement	.48*	.24*	.24*
Locus of Control	.02	.05	.03*
School Characteristics			
Public	−.17*	.03*	−.18*
Student Experiences			
Curriculum	.17*	.18*	.26*
Disciplinary Problems	−.09*	−.09*	−.06*

* Variables whose associated raw weights are at least four times their standard error

Table 53   Major determinants of being in the academic curriculum for total group
(Standardized regression weights)

Background	
Sex	−.04*
SES	.05*
Race/ethnicity	−.05*
Region	.00
Community	.02
Family Support	
Parents' Aspirations	.19*
Non-school Learning	.03
Study Aids	.02
Intact Family	−.01
Parental Role in Program Planning	.07*
Sophomore Year	
Ability & Attitudes	
Sophomore Vocabulary	.24*
Locus of Control	.05*
School Characteristics	
Public	−.08*

* Variables whose associated raw weights are at least four times their standard error

plan their school program did more homework than students whose parents had not been involved in such planning.

Disciplinary Problems

The three student educational experiences we have discussed above all facilitated higher achievement. The disciplinary problems variable has

Table 54   *Major determinants of amount of homework done for total group*
(Standardized regression weights)

Background	
Sex	−.15*
SES	.01
Race/ethnicity	−.05*
Region	.05*
Community	−.02
Family Support	
Parents' Aspirations	.05*
Non-school Learning	.00
Study Aids	.05*
Intact Family	−.02
Parental Role in Program Planning	.10*
Sophomore Year Ability & Attitudes	
Sophomore Vocabulary	−.02
Locus of Control	.05*
School Characteristics	
Public	−.00
School Experiences	
Curriculum	.06*
Number of Math Courses	.17*
Number of Science Courses	.08*
Number of Language Courses	.17*
Disciplinary Problems	−.16*

* Variables whose associated raw weights are at least four times their standard error

just the opposite effect. As is indicated in Table 55, students with disciplinary problems are most likely to be male, to have a low score on their sophomore year vocabulary test, to have parents who were not involved when the student planned his/her school program, to have little sense of control over their futures, to come from high SES families, and to attend public high school.

Looking at these results together, we see that the family factors which lead to student behaviors that facilitate learning in the last two years of high school are:

- Having high educational aspirations for the student;
- Being involved with the student in program planning;
- Providing opportunities for out-of-school learning, and
- Providing study aids in the home.

Contrary to Coleman and Hoffer's argument, we observe that coming from an intact family has no direct effect on achievement gains nor is it one of the family factors that facilitates student behaviors that lead to these achievement gains.

This portion of the analysis also shows that the amount of homework done by students is determined in large part by the courses they take and that the courses they take are determined largely by curriculum track.

Table 55   *Major determinants of disciplinary problems for total group*
(Standardized regression weights)

Background	
Sex	.17*
SES	.08*
Race/ethnicity	−.01
Region	.05*
Community	.04*
Family Support	
Parents' Aspirations	−.06*
Non-school Learning	.03
Study Aids	−.04*
Intact Family	−.04*
Parental Role in Program Planning	−.08*
Sophomore Year Ability & Attitudes	
Sophomore Vocabulary	−.12*
Locus of Control	−.08*
School Characteristics	
Public	.06

* Variables whose associated raw weights are at least four times their standard error

The primary student behavior which limits achievement gains, having disciplinary problems in school, is related to some family factors, such as no parental involvement in program planning, low parental aspirations for the student, and coming from a non-intact family.

Mathematics Gains — A Closer Look

While the overall growth in mathematics is relatively modest compared to the growth in vocabulary, there is much more variability in mathematics growth rates across the subpopulations when compared to the other achievement areas. Growth rates in both mathematics and vocabulary are related to social class, race/ethnicity, school type, and curriculum. Growth rates in science are related to race/ethnicity, school type, and curriculum. While growth in science, and to a lesser extent growth in vocabulary, show sensitivity to demographic characteristics as well as school variables, the relationships are not as strong as in the case of mathematics.

In terms of social class, members of the highest SES group show mathematics gains of 30 per cent of a standard deviation while members of the low SES group show gains of only 10 per cent of a standard deviation. Similarly Asian Americans show a 30 per cent standard deviation gain while Mexican Americans show only a 10 per cent of a standard deviation gain in mathematics. Students from

Catholic schools show 40 per cent gains while public and private school students show only 20 per cent gains in terms of standard deviation units. This latter result comes as no surprise, of course, since Coleman and his colleagues[3] have reported similar findings. With respect to curriculum, students in the vocational program show approximately one-third the gain (in standard deviation units) when compared to students in the academic program.

While comparisons of subgroups with respect to the amount of gain are of considerable interest, they tell us very little about qualitative differences in gain. For example, traditionally low scoring subgroups in the mathematics area may show the same amount of gain in terms of standard deviation units as high scoring groups, but their gains may differ with respect to the complexity of the material that has been learned.

In order to examine this possibility, four subtests of five items each were selected that appeared to reflect a hierarchy of mathematical skills. That is, each subtest consisted of items that were internally homogeneous with respect to the level of mathematical skill required. Figure 3 shows the mathematical operations required for mastery of the skills represented in each of the five item subtests. As this figure makes clear, the subtests were constructed to form a hierarchy of skills. The level 1 subtest requires the simplest of operations (arithmetic on whole numbers) while level 2 is made up of slightly more complex arithmetical operations. The brackets in this figure spanning the levels indicate that, ideally, the higher levels would require all the skills at the lower levels plus some new skill unique to that level. For the most part this hierarchy is maintained in that at least one or more of the lower level operations are involved in the solutions to items at the higher levels. The 'P' in the boxes in Figure 3 indicates the average difficulty of the items in each subtest. For example, at level 1 the P is 0.77 indicating that, on average, 77 per cent of the sophomore students got these five items correct. At the highest level (level 4), the P is 0.24 indicating that, on average, only a quarter of the sample gave correct answers to these items.

Mastery at any one of the four levels was defined as getting four out of five items at that level correct. In addition to the simple mastery score, each individual also had a 'mastery probability' score. This score was the probability that a given individual got four or more items correct at a given level. Thus any one individual had eight mastery probability scores, four (one for each test level) as a sophomore and four more as a senior. Table 56 presents the percentage of students who were defined as masters at the time of their sophomore

Figure 3: Hierarchically overlapping mathematics subtests

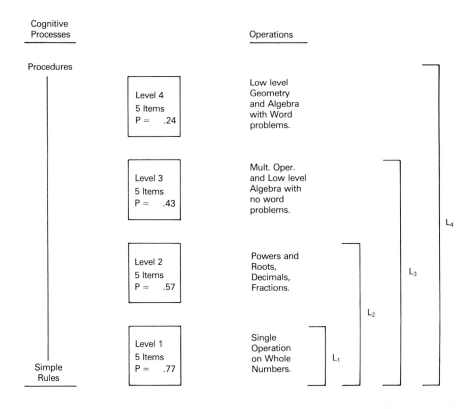

testing and then again when they became seniors. The students are subdivided by curriculum.

Inspection of Table 56 suggests that the larger increments in terms of percentage gains occur at the higher mastery levels, (e.g., see gains in the total column). This is not unexpected since mastery at levels 3 and 4 would be more sensitive to the mathematics course work normally offered during the last two years of high school. The bad news here is that less that half of the senior high school population appears to have mastered simple powers, decimals, and fractions. Of particular interest are the relatively large differences between curriculum groups at even the lowest levels of mastery (e.g., L 1). Only slightly more than one-half of the seniors who are in the vocational program appear to have mastered simple arithmetic operations. When differential gains (i.e., which group showed the biggest gains)

Table 56 *Percentage of the total students who were defined as masters in the sophomore and senior testing by curriculum group.*

Mastery (M) at each level	Sophomore				Senior				Gain as a percent of base year			
	Gen	Acad	Voc	Total	Gen	Acad	Voc	Total	Gen	Acad	Voc	Total
M at L_1	62	81	50	67	66	83	54	72	6	2	8	7
M at L_2	33	60	20	40	39	67	26	47	18	12	30	18
M at L_3	17	39	8	23	22	49	13	33	29	26	38	43
M at L_4	4	11	1	6	6	19	3	9	50	73	200	50

were investigated and statistically tested, there were no significant differences between curriculum groups except at the third and fourth levels. The academic students showed bigger gains than the general and vocational groups at the two higher levels of mathematical operations.

Differential gains were also investigated in three racial/ethnic groups: White, Black, and Hispanic. Blacks showed significantly greater gains than did the White students at the lowest mathematical level, while the Whites showed significantly greater gains at the highest level (L4). There was no significant difference between the groups at levels L2 and L3. Thus, while Blacks and Whites showed similar gains in terms of standard deviation units based on the total test score, there were substantial qualitative differences between their gains. Blacks were showing big gains in their mastery of simple arithmetical operations while Whites were showing superior gains in geometry and algebra problems.

Summary

This chapter has shown that the major determinants of student achievement gains in high school were the number of relevant courses taken, the amount of homework done, being in the academic curriculum, and not having disciplinary problems. As we saw earlier, changes in these important educational experiences were also major causes of the decline in tested achievement from 1972 to 1982.

We have seen in this chapter that these educational experiences work in a similar manner for students of different racial/ethnic backgrounds. That is, the same kinds of experiences produce the same amount of gains in tested achievement. However, a detailed analysis of gains in mathematics has shown that, although the size of the gains made by students from different racial/ethnic groups may be similar, the kinds of mathematics which these gains represent differs, primarily because of the different course-taking experience of these groups of students.

We have also seen that family structure plays no direct role in achievement gain, although it is related to the prevalance of a negative factor — student disciplinary problems. In the next chapter we will look at another, more extremely negative, behavior — dropping out of high school — and will see what factors are related to this problem.

Notes and References

1. COLEMAN, J. S. and HOFFER, T. (1987) *Public and Private High Schools: The Impact of Communities,* New York: Basic Books. pp. 119.
2. ROCK, D. A., EKSTROM, R. B., GOERTZ, M. E. and POLLACK, J. (1986) *Study of Excellence in High School Education: Longitudinal Study, 1980–82 Final Report,* CS 86-231. Washington, DC: US Government Printing Office. The raw regression weights can be found in Tables 9–19 through 9–22, pp. 353–360.
3. COLEMAN, J. S., HOFFER, T. and KILGORE, S. (1981) *High School Achievement: Public, Catholic, and Private Schools Compared.* New York: Basic Books.

7 *Who Stays in School? Who Drops Out?*

In the preceding chapters we have looked at students who persisted in high school until their senior year. However, many young people do not complete high school — they become high school dropouts.

The extent of the dropout problem is a subject of some debate. In Chapter 3 we saw evidence that the percentage of high schools with high attrition rates (20 per cent or more of students who entered grade 10 did not complete grade 12) had increased from 3.6 per cent of all high schools in 1972 to 7.5 per cent of all high schools in 1982. Data from the National Center for Education Statistics indicate that only about three-quarters of all 18 and 19-year-olds have completed high school. However, the Bureau of the Census has reported that the annual dropout rate in US high schools fell significantly between 1972 and 1982. According to these data, approximately 6.3 per cent of all students in grades 10, 11, and 12 became dropouts in 1972, but only 5.2 per cent in 1982.

Despite disagreements about the statistics, high school attrition is a growing concern among educators and policymakers. High school dropouts are estimated to have unemployment rates that are twice as high as high school graduates of the same age; dropouts are much more likely to be among the long-term unemployed. Individuals who have not completed high school earn 26 to 31 per cent less than individuals who completed high school but who have not attended college.

A version of this chapter first appeared in *Teachers College Record*, 1986, 87(3), pp. 356–73; and later in NATRIELLO, G. (1987) (Ed) *School Dropouts*, New York, Teachers College Press, pp. 52–69. Copyright Teachers College Press 1987.

In this chapter we focus on four questions:

- Who drops out of high school?
- Why does one student and not another drop out?
- What happens to dropouts during the time that their peers remain in school?
- How does dropping out affect gains in tested achievement?

Previous Research

Previous research has indicated that high school attrition is related to background, achievement and attitudes, and individual behaviors.

The two background characteristics most strongly related to dropping out are socioeconomic status and race/ethnicity. Students of lower socioeconomic status have been consistently shown to have higher dropout rates than high socioeconomic status students[1]. Dropout occurs more often among Hispanics than among Blacks, and more often among Blacks than Whites[2]. Other background factors which have been associated with dropout include coming from a single parent family[3], coming from a large family[4], and living in the South or in a large city.[5]

Low academic achievement, as indicated by low test scores and low grades, has also been consistently associated with high school attrition. Low scores on standardized tests have been found to be good predictors of dropout[6]. Academic failure, as indicated by low grades, is also consistently related to dropout[7]. Students who become dropouts have been shown to be dissatisfied with school and to have lower self-esteem[8]. Students with no plans for postsecondary education also been shown more likely to become dropouts.[9]

Student behaviors that have been found to be associated with dropout include enrollment in a non-academic (vocational or general) curriculum[10] and problem behaviors such as delinquency and truancy[11]. Other researchers have pointed out the role that employment during high school [12] and pregnancy[13] play in dropout.

Methodology

The data used in this chapter, as in the preceding chapter, are derived from the sample of approximately 30,000 High School and Beyond students who were sophomores in approximately 1000 public and private high schools in 1980. A follow-up in 1982 collected information from over 2,000 of the sophomores who had dropped out of school; these dropouts, who would have been classmates of the 1982 seniors, are the focus of this chapter.

The findings are based on three different kinds of analysis. First, descriptive analysis is used to describe who stayed in school and who dropped out of high school between the sophomore and senior years. Students who stayed in school ('stayers') are compared to those who did not complete school ('dropouts') on a number of dimensions: race/ethnicity, socioeconomic status, family structure, home educational support system, ability and attitudes, and school behaviors. Second, path analysis is used to explain why some students and not others drop out of school. Third, a value added analysis estimates the relative impact of staying in or dropping out of school on gains in tested achievement.

Who Drops Out of School?

Students who later became dropouts differed significantly in their sophomore year from those students who persisted in high school. These differences include background, educational achievement, school experiences, out-of-school activities, educational aspirations, and attitudes toward self and society. Thirty per cent of the dropouts reported leaving school during tenth grade, 44 per cent during eleventh grade, and 26 per cent during twelfth grade.

Background

Dropouts are disproportionately from low SES families and racial/ethnic minority groups. While 15 per cent of students who were sophomores in 1980 did not complete high school two years later, nearly 25 per cent of Black students dropped out. Dropouts were also more likely to be older, to be males rather than females, and to attend public schools in urban areas in the South or West.

Dropouts tended to come from homes with a weaker educational support system. Compared to stayers, dropouts: (i) had fewer study aids present in their homes; (ii) had less opportunity for non-school related learning; (iii) were less likely to have both natural parents living at home; (iv) had mothers with less formal education; (v) had parents with lower educational expectations for their children; (vi) had mothers who were more likely to be working; and (vii) had parents who were less likely to be interested in or to monitor both in-school and out-of-school activities.

Educational achievement and other school-related behaviors and attitudes

As sophomores dropouts exhibited different school behaviors than students who would persist in high school. The dropouts had lower school grades and lower test scores, did less homework, and reported more disciplinary problems in school.

It appears that the gap between stayers and dropouts is greater in the area of school performance (as measured by reported school grades) than it is in tested achievement. This suggests that motivation to succeed in school, more than ability, determines dropout. The typical sophomore who remained in school reported a grade average of 'B' while those who dropped out reported grades of 'mostly Cs', a difference of about one standard deviation. The typical dropout's grades were at approximately the sixteenth percentile of the school stayers.

The dropouts had lower sophomore year scores on all of the HS&B achievement tests than the stayers. The mean score differences were smallest in science and largest in mathematics. The dropouts' science test scores placed them at about the twenty-eighth percentile of school stayers while their mathematics scores placed them at about the twenty-third percentile of the stayers.

Not surprisingly the dropouts reported doing less homework as sophomores than did the school stayers. Dropouts reported doing an average of 2.2 hours of homework a week as sophomores compared to 3.4 hours a week reported by stayers.

The dropouts were also more likely to report having behavior problems while in school. As shown in Table 57, dropouts were more likely than stayers to have cut classes, to have had disciplinary problems, to have been suspended from school, or to have had trouble with the police. The dropouts also reported higher rates of absenteeism and tardiness than the stayers.

The future dropouts appear to feel alienated from school life. They report lower levels of participation in most extracurricular activities, especially in athletics; about 57 per cent of the stayers participated in athletics, as compared with about 42 per cent of the students who became dropouts. They are less likely to feel satisfied with the way their education is going, to be interested in school, or to like working hard in school (See Table 58). They are less likely to feel

Table 57   *Frequency of behavior problems among dropouts and stayers (Percentage Yes)*

	Sophomores who stayed in school	Sophomores who dropped out	Dropouts minus stayers
Cut classes	25	54	29*
Had disciplinary problems	16	41	25*
Suspended or put on probation	10	31	21*
Serious trouble with law	4	13	9*

* Difference significant at or beyond the .05 level

Table 58   *Attitudes difference between dropouts and stayers (Percentage True)*

	Sophomores who stayed in school	Sophomores who dropped out	Dropouts minus stayers
I am interested in school	79	60	− 19*
I am satisfied with the way my education is going	69	45	− 24*
I like to work hard in school	56	40	− 16*
I am popular with others	78	72	− 6*

* Difference significant at or beyond the .05 level

that they are popular with other students, to feel that other students see them as a good athlete, or as important. The future dropouts also feel that other students see them as troublemakers.

The future dropouts tend to choose close friends who are also alienated from school. These friends are less school-oriented than the friends of the stayers (See Table 59). The largest dropout-stayer differences in close friends involve plans to attend college and being interested in school.

Out of school behavior

Students who later became dropouts reported spending more time in their sophomore year 'riding around' or 'going on dates' than were students who stayed in school (See Table 60). Dropouts were less likely than stayers to discuss their experiences with their parents and, as indicated earlier, the parents of dropouts are reported as doing less monitoring of the students' activities both in school and out. Dropouts also reported spending less time reading than did stayers. stayers.

Sophomores who later became dropouts were less likely to participate in church and community activities for young people than

Table 59   Behaviors and attitudes of closest friend
(Percentage True)

	Sophomores who stayed in school	Sophomores who dropped out	Dropouts minus stayers
Attended classes regularly	93	82	− 11*
Is popular	88	81	− 7*
Gets good grades	83	73	− 10*
Is interested in school	69	51	− 18*
Plans to go to college	67	44	− 24*

* Difference significant at or beyond the .05 level

Table 60   Relative amount of time spent on non-school activities
(*Scale*: from 0 = rarely to 3 = every day)

	Sophomores who stayed in school		Sophomores who dropped out		Dropouts minus stayers
	Mean	SD	Mean	SD	
Meeting/Talking with Friends	2.45	0.8	2.50	0.9	.04
Thinking/Daydreaming Alone	1.91	1.2	1.76	1.2	−.15*
Reading Newspaper	1.72	1.2	1.42	1.2	−.31*
Talking with Mother/Father about personal experiences	1.26	1.2	1.03	1.1	−.23*
Driving around	1.25	1.1	1.67	1.1	.43*
Reading for pleasure	1.21	1.1	1.01	1.1	−.20*
Going on dates	1.01	0.9	1.45	1.0	.44*

* Difference significant at or beyond the .05 level

the sophomores who persisted in high school. About 40 per cent of the stayers, but only about 29 per cent of the dropouts, took part in church activities when they were high school sophomores. About 19 per cent of the future dropouts, as compared to about 25 per cent of the stayers, took part in community youth organizations.

The future dropouts were slightly more likely to be working for pay during their sophomore year (47 per cent) than were stayers (42 per cent). The dropouts reported working more hours per week than the stayers and receiving a higher hourly wage. The dropouts were more likely to report finding their current or most recent job more enjoyable than school (66 per cent) than the stayers (54 per cent). The dropouts also reported that their job was more important to them than school more often than did the stayers (23 per cent versus 10 per cent).

Taken together, these findings suggest that the sophomores who later became dropouts were finding more satisfaction and success in their employment activities than in school.

Educational expectations

As sophomores the future dropouts expected to complete less education than did the stayers. The typical stayer thought he or she would complete between two and four years of college, while the typical dropout thought he or she would finish high school and take some junior college training.

Attitudes toward self and society

Dropouts differed from stayers on many of the questionnaire items measuring self-esteem, locus of control, gender role attitudes, and life values.

Self-esteem items that focused on whether the students had a positive attitude toward themselves or felt of equal worth compared to others showed no practical or significant differences between dropouts and stayers. However, when asked if they were satisfied with themselves or if they had much to be proud of, dropouts were significantly more likely than stayers to show lower self concept.

On most of the locus of control items, dropouts responded with a significantly more externalized sense of control, indicating that they are more likely than stayers to feel that their destiny is out of their hands.

The gender role attitudes scale showed that the females who became dropouts were significantly more likely to agree with items such as 'Most women are happiest when making a home' and 'It is usually better if the man is the achiever and the woman takes care of the home' than were female stayers. This suggests that holding stereotypic views of gender roles may contribute to dropout among females, perhaps because marriage and motherhood are seen in a more idealistic light.

The contrast in life values of stayers and dropouts is shown in Table 61. Dropouts are more likely than stayers to give importance to 'getting away from this part of the country' and to 'having lots of money'.

Why Does One Student and Not Another Drop Out of School?

The preceding section describes how the future dropouts and the stayers differed in their sophomore year in high school. In this section,

Table 61   Comparison of life values of stayers and dropouts
(*Scale*: from 1 = Not Important to 3 = Very Important)

	Sophomores who stayed in school	Sophomores who dropped out	Dropouts minus stayers
Finding steady work	2.83	2.77	−.06*
Having strong friendships	2.81	2.74	−.07*
Having lots of money	2.24	2.30	.07*
Living close to parents	1.98	1.87	−.11*
Being a community leader	1.66	1.59	−.07*
Getting away from this area of the country	1.54	1.72	.18*

* Difference significant at or beyond the .05 level

the question of why one student rather than another drops out will be examined by analyzing: (i) their self-reported reasons for dropping out of school; and (ii) the results of a path analysis which provides insights into the causal factors behind high school attrition.

Reported Reasons for Dropping Out of High School

In 1982, students who dropped out of school were asked their reason(s) for leaving. The students could check as many reasons as they felt relevant. The major reasons, chosen by ten percent or more of the dropouts, are shown in Table 62, both for the group as a whole and separately for males and females.

The most frequently reported reasons for leaving school for the total group were poor grades and not liking school. This indicates that about one third of all dropouts leave high school because they do not achieve in school and/or because they are alienated from school. Males are somewhat more likely to leave school for these reasons than are females. Males are also more than twice as likely than females to report leaving high school because of behavior problems, including not being able to get along with teachers (21 per cent of male dropouts) and being expelled or suspended (13 per cent of male dropouts). Males were also more likely than females to leave high school because of economic-related issues. Fourteen per cent of the males, as contrasted to 8 per cent of the females, said they left school because they had to help support their family. Twenty-seven per cent of the males and 11 per cent of the females said they left school because they were offered a job. Females, in contrast, are more likely than males to leave high school for personal/family formation reasons. Nearly a third (31 per cent) of female dropouts report that they left

Table 62   *Major reasons for dropping out of school*
(Percentage responding 'Yes' to each item)

	Total	Males	Females
Did not like school	33	35	31
Poor grades	33	36	30
Offered job and chose to work	19	27	11
Getting married	18	7	31
Could not get along with teachers	15	21	9
Had to help support family	11	14	8
Pregnancy	11	–	23
Expelled or suspended	9	13	5

Note: Other reasons for dropping out included travel (7 per cent), inability to get into desired program, inability to get along with other students, and illness (all 6 per cent).

high school to marry and nearly a quarter (23 per cent) reported that they left school because of pregnancy.

The diversity of the reasons given for dropping out of high school, encompassing academic, behavioral, economic, and personal factors, suggests that there is no single, simple cause underlying this problem. This, in turn, led to the development of a complex path analysis model.

Path Analysis

Student self-reports provide a list of reasons for leaving school, but they do not yield much insight into the causal factors that led a student to drop out of school. A path model was developed that relates demographics, family educational support, sophomore year ability and attitudes, and student school behaviors to the student's decision to stay in or drop out of school (See Figure 4). The model contrasts Whites with Blacks, and Whites with Mexican Americans and Puerto Ricans, to identify possible differences in home educational support and in student behaviors. In addition, the model was run separately within racial/ethnic groups to determine whether the educational process works the same way for minority students as for White students.

The direct effects of the explanatory variables which had the largest standardized path coefficients, for total group or for the racial/ethnic subgroups, are shown in Table 63. Overall, having behavior problems in school was most strongly related to becoming a dropout while having good grades was most strongly related to persistence in high school.

Figure 4:   *Explanatory Model For Dropout Status*

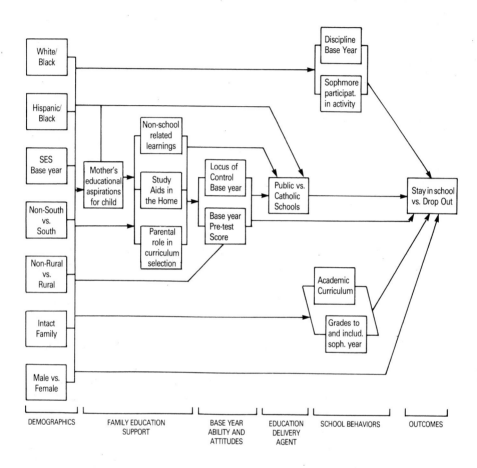

Table 63   Direct effects of explanatory variables on decision to stay in or drop out of school
(*Scale*: 0 = Dropout, 1 = Stay)

| | Standardized Regression Weights | | | |
	Total	White	Black	Hispanic
Background				
Intact family	.07*	.06*	.07	.11*
SES	.06*	.07*	.02	.08
Race/ethnicity-White	−.07*			
Race/ethnicity-Hispanic	−.04*			
Region	.03*	.06*	−.08*	−.03
Sex	.03	.04*	−.04	.06
Family Support				
Study Aids	.03	.04*	−.01	.01
Sophomore Year Ability and Attitudes				
Grades	.17*	.18*	.07	.19*
Math Test Score	.08*	.07*	.09	.02
Locus of Control	−.03	−.01	−.06	−.10*
Student Experiences				
Behavior Problems	−.22*	−.22*	−.21*	−.28*

* Variables whose associated raw weights are at least four times their standard error.

The background variables related to the decision to stay in or drop out of high school were, in approximate order of importance:

Intact family: White and Hispanic, but not Black, students who came from an intact, two parent family were less likely to drop out of school.

SES: Students of higher socioeconomic status were less likely to drop out.

Race, ethnicity: Other things being equal, Whites and Hispanics were more likely to drop out of school than Blacks. The critical control variables here are sophomore year grades and achievement test scores.

Region: Whites in the South were more likely to drop out than Whites in other regions, assuming all other variables were held constant. Blacks in the South were less likely to drop out than blacks in other regions.

Sex: White and Hispanic males were more likely to drop out than females; Black females were more likely to drop out than Black males.

The only family education support variable related to dropping out was study aids in the home. The more study aids available, the less likely White students were to drop out.

Three sophomore year ability and attitude variables were related to staying in or dropping out of school. They were:

Grades: Students with low grades were more likely to drop out. Grades appear to be more important in the dropping out decision for Whites and Hispanics than for Blacks.

Mathematics Test Score: Poor mathematics skills, as measured by the sophomore year achievement test, were related to drop-out, especially for Whites.

Locus of Control: An externalized locus of control, or the feeling that one can do little to control one's destiny, was negatively related to drop out, especially among minority students.

Having behavioral problems was also related to dropout. Students who cut classes, had disciplinary problems, had been suspended, and/or had trouble with the police were much more likely to drop out.

As indicated earlier, having behavior problems and having low grades are the major determinants of dropout. What factors affect these behaviors? The same path analysis showed several demographic and family variables were related to behavioral problems and to grades.

Behavior Problems

Students exhibiting problem behaviors, such as cutting classes and having disciplinary problems, during their sophomore year tended to be males with low verbal ability (as measured by the vocabulary test scores) and with a sense that they had little control over their lives (externalized locus of control). They tended to come from homes which failed to provide a supportive educational environment. Parents had low educational aspirations for these students and the parents were not involved in helping the student plan a high school program. The major direct effects of the demographic, family, ability and attitude variables on sophomore year problem behavior are shown in Table 64.

Grades

Self-reported grades in high school, as of the sophomore year, were highest for students with high verbal ability (as measured by the vocabulary test), who did not engage in problem behavior, and who spent more time doing homework. The typical student with high grades was a female whose family provided strong educational

Table 64 *Direct effects of explanatory variables on behavior problems, sophomore year* (*Scale*: 0 = No, 1 = Yes)

| | Standardized Regression Weights | | | |
	Total	White	Black	Hispanic
Background				
Sex	.13*	.14*	.15*	.08
SES	.05*	.04*	.02	.24*
Region	.05*	.03	.14*	.08
Community Type	.05*	.06*	.03	.00
Intact Family	−.04*	−.04*	−.02	−.08
Family Support				
Parents' Aspirations for Student	−.09*	−.08*	−.10*	−.15*
Study Aids	−.04*	−.04	−.01	−.12
Non-School Learning	.04*	.03	03	.07
Parental Role in Program Planning	−.10*	−.10*	−.13*	−.07
Sophomore Year Ability and Attitudes				
Vocabulary Test	−.14*	−.13*	−.14*	−.13*
Locus of Control	−.08*	−.08*	−.04	−.19*

* Variables whose associated raw weights are at least four times their standard error.

support (as indicated by the mother's educational aspirations for the student and by parental involvement in planning the student's high school program). These sophomores also tended to be enrolled in the academic curriculum, to do more homework, to have fewer behavior problems, to be involved in extracurricular activities, and to have an internalized locus of control. Other things being equal, grades in the South and in rural schools tended to be higher.

The major direct effects of the background, family, ability and attitude, and student experience variables on grades are shown in Table 65.

What Happened to Dropouts Between 1980 and 1982?

The HS&B follow-up survey collected information on the dropouts' activities, attitudes and experiences between the time they left high school and 1982.

At the time of the follow-up survey, 47 per cent of the dropouts were working full-time or part-time, 10 per cent were taking courses or participating in job training programs, 16 per cent were homemakers, 3 per cent were in the military service, and 29 per cent were looking for work. These percentages varied, however, by gender and by race/ethnicity. For example, more Whites and males reported working for pay than Blacks and females.

Dropouts reduced their educational expectations or plans between

Table 65   Direct effects of explanatory variables on grades in high school as of sophomore
year
(*Scale*: from 1 = Below D to 8 = Mostly A)

| | Standardized Regression Weights | | | |
	Total	White	Black	Hispanic
Background				
Sex	−.09*	−.10*	−.08*	−.04
Region	−.06*	−.05*	−.07	−.12*
Community Type	−.04*	−.03*	−.07	−.04
Intact Family	.03*	.03*	.02	.04
Family Support				
Parents' Aspirations for Student	.08*	.09*	.04	.07
Study Aids	−.03*	−.03	−.05	−.01
Parental Role in Program Planning	.06*	.06*	.03	.03
Sophomore Year Ability and Attitudes				
Vocabulary Test	.30*	.30*	.16*	.15*
Locus of Control	.07*	.07*	.06	.08
Student Experiences				
Curriculum	.08*	.07*	.07	.12*
Behavior Problems	−.21*	−.22*	−.20*	−.21*
Participation in Activities	.08*	.09*	.09*	.03
Homework	.14*	.13*	.18*	.21*

* Variables whose associated raw weights are at least four times their standard error.

1980 and 1982. As sophomores, 40 per cent reported they would be disappointed if they did not graduate from college. Two years later, this figure was 26 per cent. However, 58 per cent of the dropouts reported in 1982 that they planned to complete high school eventually. While dropouts had lowered their educational aspirations, they had an improved self-concept and, as indicated by the locus of control scale, more sense of control over life in 1982 than in 1980.

During the 1980 to 1982 period, 21 per cent of the dropouts reported they had participated in a job training program and/or educational activities other than formal educational course work. Seventeen percent had enrolled in an educational institution, and by 1982, 14 per cent reported they had obtained a GED.

A still later follow-up of these same dropouts, in 1984, showed that approximately 30 per cent of the students who dropped out either returned to high school to obtain a diploma or obtained a GED[14]. Students who dropped out late in their high school careers were more likely to complete their high school education than students who dropped out earlier. Among subpopulations, males were more likely to return to and complete high school than females and Whites were more likely to return and complete school than Blacks or Hispanics. Students from lower socioeconomic levels and students with lower tested achievement were also less likely to return and complete high school.

The Impact of Dropping Out of School on Gains in Tested Achievement

A value added analysis was carried out to estimate the relative impact of early dropout (before the end of the junior year) on achievement gains as contrasted with later dropouts and with stayers in each curriculum. The groups contrasted with the baseline, early dropout, group included:

- Late dropouts and/or early dropouts who subsequently received additional education or training, such as formal tutoring or GED work;
- School stayers in the general curriculum
- School stayers in the academic curriculum
- School stayers in the vocational curriculum

Table 66 presents the standardized adjusted gains averaged across achievement areas by various subgroups and curriculum classifications. The entries in the table indicate the gains in pretest standard deviation units by curriculum type and by racial/ethnic and sex groups.

The results clearly show that staying in school positively impacts on gains in achievement, and that staying in school in the academic or, to a lesser extent, in the general curriculum leads to larger overall gains than staying in the vocational curriculum.

The results also show that females, and to a lesser extent minorities, are relatively 'bigger losers' when they drop out of school. Blacks and females fall far behind in the language development areas of vocabulary, reading, and writing when they leave school early. Because females and minorities tend to take fewer high school courses in science and mathematics than males and Whites, the impact of dropout is less for them in these areas.

Summary

Identifying who drops out of school and why and assessing the impact of this decision on future behaviors and achievement are difficult tasks. Educators and policymakers do not share a common definition of 'dropout'. Students drop out of school for a variety of personal reasons. And the impact of leaving school is affected by when an individual drops out, what he or she does after dropping out, and the outcome measures employed.

The analyses in this chapter help our understanding of the

Table 66   Contrasts of standardized achievement gains of later dropouts and stayers with early dropouts, by test and by subgroup

By Test Status	Vocabulary	Reading	Math	Science	Writing	Total
Late dropouts	.00	.00	.00	−.01	.01	.01
Stayers — vocational	.02	.01	.02	.03	.05	.08
Stayers — general	.05	.03	.05	.05	.08	.12
Stayers — academic	.07	.05	.11	.05	.09	.16
By Subgroup Status	Male	Female	White	Black	Hispanic	
Late dropouts	.03	−.03	.02	−.01	−.06	
Stayers — vocational	.04	.12	.07	.10	.11	
Stayers — general	.08	.16	.11	.18	.16	
Stayers — academic	.13	.21	.16	.25	.16	

dropout problem. First, we have determined that the critical variables related to dropping out are school performance, as measured by grades, and extent of problem behavior.

Second, problem behavior and grades appear to be determined in part by the home educational support system. Parents' educational aspirations for the student, number of study aids in the home, parental involvement in planning the student's high school program, and the provision of opportunities for non-school learning all affect school academic performance and/or deportment.

Third, regardless of ethnicity, sex group membership, or curriculum choice, staying in school increases achievement gains in all tested areas. Students in the academic curriculum gained most, followed by students in the general and then the vocational curriculum. Females and minorities suffered the greatest losses, with respect to unrealized achievement gains, if they dropped out of school. These unrealized achievement gains for women and minorities were largest in the language developement areas of vocabulary, reading, and writing.

Notes and References

1.   ALEXANDER, K. L., ECKLAND, B. K., and GRIFFIN, L. J. (1976) 'The Wisconsin model of socioeconomic achievement: A replication', *American Journal of Sociology*, 81, 2, pp. 324–342; BACHMAN, J. G., GREEN, S., and WIRTANEN, I. D. (1971) *Youth in Transition: Dropping Out-Problem or Symptom?*, Vol. 3. Ann Arbor, Institute for Social Research, University of Michigan; BACHMAN, J. G., O'MALLEY, P. J., and JOHNSON, J. (1971) *Youth in Transition: Adolescence to Adulthood-Change and Stability in the Lives of Young Men*, Vol 6. Ann Arbor:

Institute for Social Research, University of Michigan; CAMP, C.
(1980) *School Dropouts*, Sacramento: Assembly Office of Research,
California Legislature (ERIC Document Reproduction Service No.
ED 191 959); CHILDREN'S DEFENSE FUND (1974) *Children Out of School in
America*, Cambridge, MA: Author; COMBS, J. and COOLEY, W. W.
(1968) 'Dropouts in high school and after school' *American Educational
Research Journal*, 5, 3, pp 343–363; HOWARD, M. A. P. and ANDERSON,
R. J. (1978) 'Early identification of potential dropouts: A literature
review', *Child Welfare* 57, 4, pp. 221–231; HOYT, K. B. (1962) 'The
counselor and the dropout', *The Clearinghouse* 36, 9, pp. 515–522;
LLOYD, D. N. (1978) 'Prediction of school failure from third-grade
data', *Educational and Psychological Measurement* 38, pp. 1193–1200;
MARE, R. D. (1980) 'Social background and school continuation deci-
sions', *Journal of the American Statistical Association*, 75, pp. 295–305;
PALLAS, A. M. (1984) *The determinants of high school dropout*, Unpublished Doctoral Dissertation, Department of Sociology, Johns Hopkins
University, Baltimore; RUMBERGER, R. W. (1983) 'Dropping out of high
school: The influence of race, sex, and family background', *American
Educational Research Journal*, 20, 2, pp. 199–220; SCHRIBER, D. (1962)
'The school dropout — Fugitive from failure', *The Bulletin of the Na-
tional Association of Secondary School Principals* 46, 274, pp. 233–241;
STEINBERG, L., BLINDE, P. L. and CHAN, K. S. (1984) 'Dropping out
among language minority youth', *Review of Educational Research* 54,
pp. 113–132; STICE, G. and EKSTROM, R. B. (1964) *High school attrition*
(Research Bulletin No RB–64–53). Princeton, NJ: Educational Testing
Service; STROUP, A. L. and ROBINS, L. N. (1972) 'Research notes: Ele-
mentary school predictors of high school dropout among black males',
Sociology of Education, 45, pp. 212–222.
2. BROWN, G. H., ROSEN, N. L., HILL, S. T. and OLIVAS, M. A. (1980)
The Condition of Education for Hispanic Americans (National Center for
Education Statistics). Washington, DC: Government Printing Office;
Rumberger (1983) *Op. cit.*; US BUREAU OF THE CENSUS (1982)
'School enrollment — Social and economic characteristics of students:
October, 1981', *Current Population Reports* 20, 373.
3. NEILL, S. B. (1979) *Keeping Students in School: AASA Critical Issue
Report*, Arlington, VA: American Association of School Admini-
strators; Rumberger (1983) *Op. cit.*
4. Rumberger (1983) *Op. cit.*
5. Stice and Ekstrom (1964) *Op. cit.*
6. Alexander *et al.*, (1976) *Op. cit.*; Combs and Cooley, (1968) *Op. cit.*;
COOK, E. S. (1956) 'An analysis of factors related to withdrawal from
high school prior to graduation', *Journal of Educational Research* 30,
3, pp. 191–196; Lloyd (1978) *Op. cit.*; Pallas, (1984) *Op. cit.*; PENTY,
R. C. (1956) *Reading Ability and High School Dropouts*, New York:
Teachers College Press, Columbia University; Stice and Ekstrom (1964)
Op. cit; WALTERS, H. E. and KRANZLER, G. D. (1970) 'Early identifica-
tion of the school dropout' *School Counselor* 18, 2, pp. 97–104.
7. Bachman, Green and Wirtanen (1971) *Op. cit.*; CERVANTES, L. F. (1965)
The Dropouts: Causes and Cures, Ann Arbor: University of Michigan

Press; Pallas (1984) *Op. cit.*; Steinberg, Blinde and Chan (1984) *Op. cit.*; Stice and Ekstrom (1964) *Op. cit.*

8. Bachman, Green and Wirtanen (1971) *Op. cit.*; Bachman, O'Malley and Johnson (1971) *Op. cit.*; Cervantes (1965) *Op. cit.*; HUNT, N. and WOODS, J. (1979) *Interrupted Education: Students Who Drop Out.* Brooklyn: New York City Board of Education (ERIC Document Reproduction Service No. ED 181 44); LUCAS, I. (1971) *Puerto Rican Dropouts in Chicago* (Final Report Project No. O-E-108), Chicago: Council on Urban Education.; TAKESIAN, S.A. (1967) *A Comparative Study of the Mexican-American Graduate and Dropout.* Unpublished Doctoral Dissertation. University of Southern California, Los Angeles; YUDIN, L. W., RING, S., NOWAKIWSKA, M. and HEINEMANN, S. (1973) 'School dropout or college bound: Study in contrast', *Journal of Educational Research*, 67, 2, pp. 85–95.

9. Stice and Ekstrom (1964) *Op. cit.*

10. Stice and Ekstrom (1964) *Op. cit.*

11. Bachman, Green and Wirtanen (1971) *Op. cit.*; Bachman, O'Mal, y and Johnson, (1971) *Op. cit.*; Camp, (1980) *Op. cit.*; CARNEGIE COUNCIL ON POLICY STUDIES IN HIGHER EDUCATION (1979) *Giving Youth a Better Chance: Options for Education, Work and Service*, San Francisco: Jossey-Bass; ELLIOT, D. and VOSS, H. (1974) *Delinquency and Dropouts* Lexington, MA: Lexington Books; Lucas (1971) *Op. cit.*; NATRIELLO, G. (1982) *Organizational Evaluation Systems and Student Disengagement in Secondary Schools*, Final Report to the National Institute of Education. St. Louis, MO: Washington University; NATRIELLO, G., (1984) 'Problems in the evaluation of students and student disengagement from secondary schools', *Journal of Research and Development in Education*, 17, pp. 14–24; Neil (1979) *Op. cit.*; Pallas (1984); QUAY, H. C. and ALLEN, L. B. (1982) 'Truants and dropouts', *Encyclopedia of Educational Research*, New York: The Free Press, pp. 1958–1962; ROBINS, L. N. and RATICLIFFE, K. S. (1980) 'The long term outcome of truancy', in HERSOV L. and BERG I. (Eds) *Out of School: Modern Perspectives in Truancy and School Refusal*, New York: John Wiley, pp. 65–83.

12. STEINBERG, L., GREENBERGER, E., GARDUQUE, L., and McAULIFFE, S. (1982) 'High school students in the labor force: Some costs and benefits to schooling and learning', *Educational Evaluation and Policy Research*, 4, 3, pp. 363–372.

13. Camp (1980) *Op. cit.*; CENTER FOR HUMAN RESOURCES RESEARCH (1980) *The National Longitudinal Studies Handbook* Columbus, OH: Center for Human Resource Research, Ohio State University; Children's Defense Fund (1974) *Op. cit.*; Combs and Cooley (1968) *Op. cit.*; Elliot and Voss (1974) *Op. cit.*; Lucas (1971) *Op. cit.*; Rumberger (1983) *Op. cit.*; WAITE, L. J. and MOORE, K. A. (1978) 'The impact of early first birth on young women's educational attainment', *Social Forces* 56, pp. 845–865.

14. KOLSTAD, A. J. and OWINGS, J. A. (1986) 'High school dropouts who change their minds about school'. Paper presented at the annual meeting of the American Educational Research Association, San Francisco: CA.

PART 4
POLICY IMPLICATIONS

8   *Policy Recommendations for the Next Decade*

In the introduction to this book, we identified a number of policy issues in the areas of educational excellence, equity and choice that have been raised by the education reform movement of the 1980s. Has the quality of education in the American high school deteriorated? Why are students dropping out of high school? What factors contribute to academic achievement in the high school? Do all students have equal access to learning opportunities that encourage educational attainment? How do educational experiences differ in public and private schools? What can schools do to retain more students? In the following pages, we use the findings presented throughout the book to answer these questions. We conclude with a set of general policy recommendations designed to increase both equity and excellence in American schools.

Has the Quality of Education in the American High School Deteriorated?

The education reform movement was driven in large part by a perception that the rigor and quality of the educational program in American schools had deteriorated in the 1960s and 1970s. Our examination of changes in high school seniors' school experiences and in school characteristics between 1972 and 1982 generally supports this contention.

In spite of increased educational aspirations, many high school students shifted out of the academic curriculum into the less demanding general education and vocational education curricular tracks during this period of time. This shift was particularly evident among White and high and middle SES students, and was generally confined to the public sector. Black, Mexican American and Asian American students and students enrolled in non-public schools tended not to change curriculum tracks. At the same time, and probably as a result of enrolling in less rigorous programs, the average high school senior in 1982 took fewer semesters of the 'New Basics'— English, social studies, mathematics, science and foreign languages — and more vocational education courses in grades 10–12 than the typical senior in 1972. The largest declines in course-taking occurred in science and foreign languages, subject areas generally not protected by state high school course work mandates and areas in which postsecondary educational institutions had tended to relax entrance requirements during the 1970s. Some students also reported doing less homework in 1982 than in 1972. At the school level, drop out rates and teacher turnover rates were growing and the reputation of schools in the community was declining.

Our data also show, however, that the educational experiences of certain groups of students — those who remained in the academic curriculum, those enrolled in Catholic schools, and those from high SES families — did not undergo as much negative change as other students. For example, mathematics course-taking increased among students enrolled in an academic curriculum and students in Catholic high schools, while other subgroups and the total population showed declines in the amount of mathematics instruction they received. Although all groups of students took fewer science courses in 1982 than in 1972, the size of the decline was far smaller for high SES students, students in the academic curriculum and Catholic high schools students. While there was little change in the amount of time the typical high school senior spent on homework each week, high SES students showed a significant increase across the decade in time devoted to homework. Academic curriculum students also showed an increase in time spent on homework while, in contrast, the bulk of the students who were in the general and vocational curriculum spent less time. Finally, students from the most affluent families and students attending non-public schools reported much greater increases in teacher interest in students and in the quality of academic instruction than other groups of students, and, unlike students in other kinds of schools, reported no decline in their schools' reputations in the community at large.

Who Drops Out of High School and Why?

As discussed in the preceding chapter, students who dropped out after their sophomore year in high school in 1980 were disproportionately from low SES families and racial/ethnic minority groups, came from homes that provided lower levels of educational support, had lower eductional aspirations, had lower grades and lower test scores, did less homework, and reported more disciplinary problems in school. The most common explanations for leaving school by students of both sexes were poor grades and a dislike of school. Female students also cited marriage and/or pregnancy as reasons for dropping out; males were more likely than females to leave for economic reasons.

Our analyses of causal factors confirmed that having behavior problems and low grades were major factors related to the decision to drop out out of school. Problem behaviors and low grades, however, appeared to be determined in part by a weak family educational support system — few study aids in the home, low educational aspirations for the student, and lack of parent involvement in helping the student plan a high school program. Other things being equal, i.e., when students were equated on background and performance, White and Hispanic students were more likely to leave school than Blacks.

What Factors Contribute to Academic Achievement in High School?

Critics of American public elementary and secondary education in the 1980s pointed to evidence of less rigorous educational programs, lower expectations for students and insufficient time spent on school work as contributing to the test score decline of the 1970s and the growing inability of American students to compete with their peers abroad. Our analyses of the changes in the tested achievement of high school seniors between 1972 and 1982 and gains in tested achievement of students between their sophomore and senior years in high school point to a group of behaviors and processes that contribute to academic achievement at the high school level.

Home Educational Support

A student's home educational support system is an important factor in explaining cognitive growth of high school students. Mothers' educational aspirations for their children had a positive direct impact on gains in vocabulary, mathematics and writing, while nonschool learning opportunities (such as travel, trips to museums, and so on) had a small positive direct impact on gains in vocabulary and in science. In general, home educational support indirectly affected achievement gains by influencing students' behaviors in school, which, in turn, had direct impacts on gains.

The importance of a positive home environment on achievement was shown by the major contribution of home support variables in *resisting* the test score decline of the 1970s. In the case of the vocabulary test, for example, the cross-sectional analysis indicated that the 0.79 point score decline might have been 0.24 of a score point greater had there been no change in the home educational support system between 1972 and 1982.

Student Educational Experiences

Students' school experiences were the primary contributor to the score decline in the NLS/HS&B tests. The specific changes that contributed to the test score decline were fewer students enrolling in the academic curriculum, students taking fewer semesters of science and foreign language courses, and students spending less time on homework.

These same variables — curricular track, course exposure and homework — also made positive contributions to achievement gains between the sophomore and senior years in high school. In each achievement area tested, the number of courses that a student took beyond the remedial or functional level was positively related to test score gains. Students enrolled in the academic curriculum showed greater gains than did students enrolled in the general curriculum, and both groups did better than students in the vocational curriculum. This was due primarily to variations in course-taking behavior by students in the different curricula. Finally, other things being equal, students who did more homework showed greater test score gains.

School Processes

Changes in school processes between 1972 and 1982 made a small contribution to the test score decline. The changes that had the greatest impact included increases in the proportion of students rating the school as needing more academic emphasis, increases in the proportion of schools with a high dropout rate, decreases in the amount of homework done by students and decreases in the average number of foreign language and laboratory courses taken by students in a school.

The academic emphasis of schools, school climate and students' rating of their schools also contributed to achievement gains during students' high school careers. Gains were greater in schools where a large percentage of students were enrolled in the academic curriculum and in schools that offered a large number of courses in the New Basics. Students also showed larger achievement gains in schools that reported fewer disciplinary problems and where lack of parental interest in the school was not considered a problem. Finally, achievement growth was positively related to students' ratings of their teachers and their instruction.

Summary

In summary, schools do make a difference. Students who stay in school, particularly in an academic curriculum, take a large number of courses in the New Basics, and attend a school with a strong emphasis and a positive school climate achieve more than individuals who drop out or who continue in a less demanding educational program or school. *Other things being equal, these school factors have a similar impact on achievement for all groups of students, whether White or minority, male or female, enrolled in a public or in a Catholic school.*

Schools are especially effective in reducing differential achievement gains in reading and in mathematics, content areas that are most sensitive to formal schooling. It appears that programs emphasizing basic skills in reading and, to a somewhat lesser extent, mathematics have been effective in reducing the achievement gap between White and minority students and between students of different socioeconomic levels.

Do All Students Have Access to Learning Opportunities That Encourage Educational Attainment?

Unfortunately, access to those school processes that contribute to educational attainment differs by school sector and by the socio-economic composition of the student body. Beneficial school processes are more likely to be found in a Catholic than in a public school. Students who attend schools with a low SES student population are exposed to a different set of educational opportunities than are students who attend school with students from more affluent families.

Table 67 compares Catholic and public schools on a number of those measures that we found contributed to achievement gains: percentage of students in the academic curriculum, course-taking patterns, homework behaviors, dropout rates, proportion of college-bound students, availability of advanced placement courses, extent of disciplinary problems and parental interest and students' ratings of teacher interest and academic instruction in their schools. Catholic schools have higher ratings on all measures.

Nearly three-quarters of high school seniors attending Catholic schools were enrolled in the academic curriculum; not surprisingly, almost 80 per cent of all Catholic schools sent 70 per cent or more of their students on to two- or four-year colleges. This emphasis on preparing students to pursue postsecondary education is reflected in course requirements and student course-taking and homework behaviors. Nearly two-thirds of the Catholic high schools reported they required students in the college preparatory program to take four or more semesters of mathematics and science and two or more semesters of a foreign language and nearly one-half the schools participated in the advanced placement program. The average Catholic high school senior took nearly three semesters of a foreign language, four semesters of science and five semesters of mathematics in his or her last three years in school. These students also reported doing more than six hours of homework a week.

In contrast, public schools provided a much wider choice of curriculum. Only one-third of high school seniors were enrolled in the academic curriculum. Another 37 per cent were in the general education curriculum and 30 per cent in the vocational curriculum. Only eight per cent of public high schools sent 70 per cent or more of their students on to college. Since course-taking requirements are less rigorous for non-academic curricular tracks, it is not surprising that the average public high school senior took less mathematics, science and foreign language, took more semesters of vocational education courses and did about one and one-half hours less homework. Course work requirements for the college preparatory curriculum, however, were often less stringent in the public shcools. Only one-third of the public high schools required four or more semesters of mathematics and science and 12 per cent required students to take two or more semesters of a foreign language. About one-third of the schools offered advanced placement courses.

Table 67   Comparison of Catholic and public high schools 1982

	Catholic High Schools	Public High Schools
Student Eductional Experiences		
Percentage students in academic curriculum	71.4	34.6
Average number of semesters of:		
English	5.87	5.62
Social studies	5.17	4.94
Mathematics	4.67	3.59
Science	3.91	2.88
Foreign language	2.77	1.30
Vocational education	3.60	5.86
Hours of homework weekly	6.30	4.80
School Characteristics		
Percentage of schools with 70% or more college-bound students	79.0	8.0
Percentage of schools with advanced placement programs	47.7	33.7
Percentage of schools with 20% or higher dropout rate	0.7	6.5
Occurrence of verbal confrontation among students	3.34*	2.72*
Occurrence of verbal confrontation between students/teachers	3.50*	3.09*
Extent of lack of parental interest in students' progress	3.04**	2.41**
Student ratings of teacher interest in students	3.12***	2.67***
Student ratings of quality of academic instruction	3.15***	2.80***

*   1 = daily; 4 = rarely or never happens
**   1 = serious; 4 = no problem
*** 1 = poor; 4 = excellent

Catholic schools also tended to have more positive school climates than public high schools. Almost no Catholic high schools reported a dropout rate of 20 per cent or greater, compared to 6 per cent of public schools. Catholic schools were also less likely to have incidences of verbal confrontation among students or between students and teachers and less likely to report that lack of parental interest was a moderate or serious problem. Catholic school students rated teacher interest and the quality of academic instruction more highly than their public school counterparts.

While these contrasts between Catholic and public high schools help explain performance differentials between these two groups of students, Catholic high schools educate fewer than ten percent of the

United States' high school students. A policy question of even greater importance is whether access to beneficial school processes differs among the 90 per cent of the students who attend public high schools. In an attempt to answer this question, we compared student educational experiences and school characteristics in public high schools with high and low socioeconomic status student bodies.

Table 68 presents the same categories as Table 67. The contrasts between high and low SES high schools are as stark, and sometimes more so, than those we saw between Catholic and public high schools. Like Catholic high schools, high SES public schools have a strong academic emphasis. Sixty percent of the students attending high SES schools are enrolled in the academic curriculum compared to only 21 per cent in the low SES schools. Sixty percent of the high SES schools send 70 per cent or more of their students on to college; only a handful (2 per cent) of low SES high schools do the same. Students in the high SES schools take more semesters of the New Basics and fewer in vocational education, do nearly two hours more homework a week, and are four times as likely to attend a school that offers advanced placement courses. Mathematics and foreign language course requirements in the college preparatory track are also more stringent in the wealthier schools than in the low SES schools; science requirements are similar, however.

High SES schools also report fewer disciplinary problems and a higher level of parental interest in students' progress than low SES schools. Students attending high SES schools gave somewhat higher ratings for teacher interest and the quality of academic instruction that students attending the poorest schools. High SES schools were also one half as likely as low SES schools to have high dropout rates.

Who attends low SES schools? Blacks and other minority students are nearly four times as likely to attend these schools as are White students. In 1980, 12 per cent of the White and 46 per cent of the Black, Mexican American and Puerto Rican high school sophomores were enrolled in low SES schools. In contrast, 30 per cent of the White and only 10 per cent of the minority students attended schools with a high average SES student population.

In summary, schools do make a positive contribution to high school students' cognitive growth. The school factors that make a difference are as likely to be found in high SES public high schools as in Catholic schools. Unfortunately, less than one-half of the country's youngsters attend such schools. And, those who do tend to be predominately White, as well as economically well-off.

Table 68   Comparison of low and high SES high schools 1982

	High SES Schools	Low SES Schools
Student Eductional Experiences		
Percentage students in academic curriculum	61.8	21.2
Average number of semesters of:		
English	5.70	5.67
Social studies	5.04	4.92
Mathematics	4.41	3.08
Science	3.75	2.46
Foreign language	2.33	0.78
Vocational education	3.69	7.02
Hours of homework weekly	5.95	4.00
School Characteristics		
Percentage of schools with 70% or more college-bound students	61.5	2.4
Percentage of schools with advanced placement programs	64.8	16.6
Percentage of schools with 20% or higher dropout rate	6.8	12.8
Occurrence of verbal confrontation among students	3.07*	2.70*
Occurrence of verbal confrontation between students/teachers	3.28*	3.12*
Extent of lack of parental interest in students' progress	2.96**	2.21**
Student ratings of teacher interest in students	2.87***	2.62***
Student ratings of quality of academic instruction	3.00***	2.72***

*   1 = daily; 4 = rarely or never happens
**   1 = serious; 4 = no problem
***   1 = poor; 4 = excellent

Policy Recommendations for the Next Decade

What kinds of policies do the findings in this book suggest? Educational policies should be directed toward improving schools and toward equalizing access to educational opportunities for *all* students. In particular, these policies should address the high school curriculum, including special programs; access to educational programs and services; the role of the family in supporting learning; and the dropout problem.

High School Curriculum

Our study suggests that more course work in non-remedial level courses in mathematics, science and foreign languages contributes to higher scores on the kinds of vocabulary, reading and mathematical skills measured by the NLS/HS&B test battery. Therefore, we support the recommendations of the National Commission on Excellence in Education and other commissions and committees and the actions taken by many states and localities to insure that all students receive solid preparation in the 'New Basics' — English, mathematics, science, history and other social studies, and computer science. It was interesting to find that in 1982 fewer than 20 per cent of the high schools required three or more years of mathematics and three or more years of science in their *college preparatory* program — the minimum recommended by the National Commission on Excellence in Education for *all* students.

In addition to the New Basics, students entering high school at an educational disadvantage should also receive remedial services. It appears from the NLS/HS&B data and from trends in the NAEP achievement data that programs emphasizing basic skills in reading and, to a somewhat lesser extent, in mathematics, have been effective in halting much of the growth of the achievement gap between White and minority students and between students of different socioeconomic levels. Yet, while contrasts of racial/ethnic group gains in total mathematics scores show few differences, qualitative differences remain between the groups. For example, Blacks showed larger gains in items measuring basic arithmetic operations while Whites showed greater gain on test items measuring algebra and geometry skills. Schools must give consideration to how students can obtain both basic skills and subject matter competencies in a four-year program. Policymakers must also be sensitive to the competing curricular demands on students in the vocational education curriculum or in other programs designed to prepare high school students for the world of work.

Schools should also provide more frequent opportunities for students to write and to participate in laboratory courses. Since students in all curricular areas in this study were critical of the lack of academic emphasis in their course work and of the quality of the instruction, we also suggest that course content and instructional methods be reviewed and upgraded, as necessary, to ensure more rigorous content.

Access to Educational Programs and Services

All students should have an equal opportunity to take advanced academic offerings, such as honors and advanced placement courses, calculus or other advanced mathematics courses, specialized science courses, and so on. These opportunities could be provided in one of three ways: (1) Curricular offerings could be enriched in all schools so that students attending low SES schools have the same educational opportunities as students attending other schools. (2) In large communities, magnet schools could be created to provide specialized academic programs. (3) Students could receive financial support (e.g., vouchers) to attend those public or private secondary schools or postsecondary institutions that already offer advanced academic courses.

The first approach may not be cost-effective, since these kinds of courses may be of interest to only a limited number of students in any school. Under the second and third approaches, however, only a limited number of students could have physical access to advanced academic programs. In addition, approaches that remove the most academically able students from the neighborhood high school could have negative consequences for the overall quality of instruction in the neighborhood school. For example, it might be difficult to attract good teachers for those schools whose student body consists primarily of non-college bound students.

Regardless of the educational program offered, the best learning conditions and largest achievement gains are found in schools that set high expectations for their students (including the amount of homework required) and that maintain a positive school climate.

Family Educational Support System

This study has also shown the important role that families play in encouraging learning. Policies should be developed to strengthen the home educational support system, parental interest in the school and in the student's educational progress, and in providing a place to study and opportunities for non-school learning experience. Policies should also be developed to help students gain the understanding that they can influence their future through their own educational efforts.

The Dropout Problem

The dropout problem has become a subject of growing debate and activity in the United States. Congress is considering a 'Dropout Prevention and Re-entry Act' that will authorize federal funds for dropout-plagued school systems. Several states have enacted programs targeted at students who are considered at risk of leaving school because of a record of academic failure, poor school attendance or behavior problems, and/or targeted at retrieving students who have already dropped out. Underlying these actions is the belief that schools, especially when working with community groups and businesses, can prevent students from dropping out of school and/or can bring youngsters back into the educational system until they complete their high school education.

This flurry of activity has its critics, however. Finn,[1] for example, argues that school-based solutions to the dropout problem will succeed only if the causes of dropping out are school related. As he found no 'fully satisfactory 'causal' research relating [dropping out] to school factors ... the symptom is not likely to be eradicated by school-based remedies'.[2] Finn continues:

> To be sure, the most frequently cited reasons for leaving were associated with school itself. ... But being school-related does not mean that they are school-caused. They may have their origins in the individual, his family, or social class.[3]

We disagree with this assessment. First, a reciprocal relationship exists between the personal and social characteristics of students and the characteristics of the schools they attend. 'The background characteristics of students determine the kinds of schools and educational processes to which they have access, and the characteristics of schools play a role in attracting students with certain characteristics'.[4] Thus, low SES and minority students, those with the greatest propensity to drop out of school, generally attend schools with structural conditions that contribute to the dropout problem — low-achieving student bodies, over-crowded facilities, staff attitudes and actions toward the problem, and lack of funds to reduce class size or bring back long-term absentees, truants, or dropouts.[5]

Second, educational policies can be developed that address student problems with origins outside the schoolhouse door. Programs such as Head Start, Chapter 1 and bilingual education are designed to treat educational problems that arise from a family's economic or linguistic situation. We feel schools can, and should, respond constructively to students who are 'at risk' of dropping out of school.

No single program or policy can meet the needs of the diverse dropout population, however. Students drop out of high school for different reasons and at different points in their high school career. Our analyses of the dropout problem point toward several major types of programs: (i) programs to help pregnant teenagers and teenage parents remain in school; (ii) programs to help youth with economic needs combine work and education; and (iii) programs, such as alternative schools, directed toward students who perform poorly because they are dissatisfied with the school environment.

For some students, however, dropout prevention programs at the high school level come too late. Programs should be started when students first exhibit characteristics associated with high school attrition — low self-esteem, poor grades, attendance problems, and/or lack of family educational support. The student's home environment has a critical, although indirect, impact on the decision to leave school. Therefore, policies should be developed to help parents increase their interest in and monitoring of their children's school progress. Family-school cooperation should be an integral part of dropout prevention at all grades.

Notes and References

1. FINN, C. E., Jr. (1987) 'The high school dropout puzzle', *The Public Interest*, No. 87, spring, pp. 3–22.
2. *Ibid.*, pp. 14–15.
3. *Ibid.*, p. 15.
4. NATRIELLO, G., PALLAS, A. M. and McDILL, E. L. (1986) 'Taking stock: Renewing our research agenda on the causes and consequences of dropping out' in NATRIELLO, G. (Ed) *School Dropouts: Patterns and Policies*, New York, Teachers College Press.
5. FINE, M. (1986) 'Why urban adolescents drop into and out of public high school' in Natriello (1986) *Op. cit.*

Index

academic achievement   10–16,
    135–7
  family background and 13, 90,
    103–4, 106, 135–6
  grades 71–2, 92–5
  growth 89–111
    determinants of   96–103
    explanation of   95–6
    in mathematics   107–10
  in tests   72–5
  school characteristics and   13–
    16, 136–7, 137–41
  school experiences and   13, 103–
    7, 136
  student demographics and   11–
    13, 77
  see also test score decline

Catholic schools   15, 137–40
choice
  see parental choice
Coleman, J.S. et al   8, 11, 15, 108
Coleman, J.S. and Hoffer, T.   15,
    90, 106
Cooperative Institutional Research
    Program   38
course-taking   60–7, 104, 105
curriculum   57–60, 104, 105, 142
  see also extracurricular activities

demographics   11–13, 26–8
dropouts   43–4, 88, 113–28, 135,
    144–5
  academic achievement   116–17,

    124–5, 127
  attitudes   119
  backgrounds   114, 115–16
  educational expectations   119
  in 1980–82   125–7
  out-of-school behavior   117–18
  path analysis of   121–5
  self-reported reasons   120–1

education reform movement of
    1980s   133–4
  context of   4–10
educational programs
  access to   137–41, 143
  between 1972 and 1982   48–52
Ekstrom, R.B.   59, 60, 66
  see also Lee and Ekstrom
Equality of Educational
    Opportunity study   11
equity   7–9
ethnic groups   12
  see also minority students
excellence   4–7
  international comparisons   6–7
extracurricular activities   67–8,
    91–2

family characteristics   13, 28–31
  academic achievement and   135–
    6
  achievement growth and   90,
    103–4, 106
  policy recommendations on   143
Finn, C.E.   144

146